Grade 7

Addison-Wesley Mathematics

Building Thinking Skills Workbook

▲▼ **Addison-Wesley Publishing Company**

Menlo Park, California ■ Reading, Massachusetts ■ New York
Don Mills, Ontario ■ Wokingham, England ■ Amsterdam ■ Bonn
Sydney ■ Singapore ■ Tokyo ■ Madrid ■ San Juan

ISBN 0-201-27719-0

ABCDEFGHIJKL-HC-96543210

Table of Contents

Expanded Addition and Subtraction

Add the numbers using expanded notation. Then verify your
answers by adding the standard numerals.

Example:

$$573 = (5 \times 100) + (7 \times 10) + (3 \times 1)$$
$$+\ 206 = + (2 \times 100) + (0 \times 10) + (6 \times 1)$$
$$= [(5+2) \times 100] + [(7+0) \times 10] + [(3+6) \times 1]$$
$$= (\underline{7} \times 100) + (\underline{7} \times 10) + (\underline{9} \times 1) = \mathbf{779}$$

1. $\quad 841 =$ _____

$\quad +\ 156 =$ _____

$\qquad\quad =$ _____

$\qquad\quad =$ _____ $=$ _____

2. $\quad 7,039 =$ _____

$\quad +\ 2,850 =$ _____

$\qquad\quad =$ _____

$\qquad\quad =$ _____ $=$ _____

3. $\quad 654 =$ _____

$\quad -\ 23 =$ _____

$\qquad\quad =$ _____

$\qquad\quad =$ _____ $=$ _____

4. $\ 34,218 =$ _____

$\quad -\ 4,106 =$ _____

$\qquad\quad =$ _____

$\qquad\quad =$ _____ $=$ _____

The Adding Times

Look at each addition problem and complete the related equations.

1. $28 + 28 + 28 = 84$

    _____ × _____ = 84

    $84 + 28 =$ _____ × 28

    $84 + 28 + 28 =$ _____ × 28

2. $9 + 9 + 9 + 9 + 9 + 9 = 54$

    _____ × _____ = 54

    $54 + 9 =$ _____ × 9

    $54 + 9 + 9 + 9 =$ _____ × 9

3. $5 + 5 + 5 + 5 = 20$

    _____ × _____ = 20

    $20 + 5 + 5 =$ _____ × _____

    $20 + 5 + 5 + 5 + 5 =$ _____ × _____

4. $17 + 17 + 17 + 17 + 17 = 85$

    _____ × _____ = 85

    $85 + 17 + 17 + 17 =$ _____ × _____

    $85 + 17 + 17 + 17 + 17 + 17$

    $=$ _____ × _____

5. $4 + 4 + 4 + 4 + 4 + 4 + 4 = 28$

    _____ × _____ = 28

    $28 + 4 + 4 + 4 + 4 =$ _____ × _____

    $28 + 4 + 4 + 4 + 4 + 4 + 4 + 4$

    $=$ _____ × _____

6. $11 + 11 + 11 + 11 = 44$

    _____ × _____ = 44

    $44 + 11 + 11 =$ _____ × _____

    $44 + 11 + 11 + 11 + 11 + 11$

    $=$ _____ × _____

Use related operations to solve these problems.

7. Eric earns \$3 an hour for baby-sitting. In one week he

baby-sits for 15 hours. How much money does he earn? _____

8. Another week Eric earned \$51.

How many hours did he baby-sit that week? _____

Operation Orderly

Organize the **operations** so that each equation is correct. Use each
symbol only once per equation.

1. − ÷ × ( )

18	6	3	5 = 30
18	6	3	5 = 8
18	6	3	5 = 31
18	6	3	5 = 20

2. − + ×

21   (6   2)   9 = 18

21   (6   2)   9 = 24

21   6   2   9 = 133

21   6   (2   9) = 9

Organize the **numbers** so that each equation is correct.
Use each number only once per equation.

3. 12   2   4   3

(____ ÷ ____ − ____) × ____ = 6

(____ ÷ ____ − ____) × ____ = 0

(____ ÷ ____ − ____) × ____ = 8

(____ ÷ ____ − ____) × ____ = 3

4. 20   4   5   10

(____ − ____) × ____ ÷ ____ = 2

(____ − ____) × ____ ÷ ____ = 25

(____ − ____) × ____ ÷ ____ = 6

(____ − ____) × ____ ÷ ____ = 8

Organize the numbers **and** the operations so that each
equation is correct. Use each choice only once per equation.

5. 18   9   3   6   +   ×   ÷

_____ = 20

_____ = 30

_____ = 111

_____ = 15

6. 36   18   12   6   −   +   (   )   ÷

_____ = 45

_____ = 15

_____ = 22

_____ = 41

Name _____

Use Your Answer

Solve.

1. Eileen used the computer twice as long as
Doug did. If the total time they used the computer
was 24 minutes, how long did Eileen use it? _____

2. Carrie sold 14 cans of paint. She sold 4 more
than twice the number of cans that Joe sold.
How many cans of paint did Joe sell? _____

3. There are 27 female gymnasts and 5 male gymnasts
in a training session. If they are separated into 4
equal-size groups, how many are in each group? _____

4. You have two $20 bills and one $10 bill.
How much change will you receive after you
purchase 8 theater tickets that cost $6 each? _____

5. A class aquarium had 3 pairs of guppies added to the 5 pairs
already there. If half of the fish were then sold and half of the
remaining fish were given away, how many would be left? _____

Use the answers from the problems above in the
equations below, then evaluate. Correct answers will
balance these equations.

6. Prob. 1 ans. – (Prob. 2 ans. × 2) = 6

_____ – (_____ × 2) = 6

7. (Prob. 1 ans. – Prob. 2 ans.) × 2 = 22

(_____ – _____) × 2 = 22

8. (Prob. 3 ans. ÷ Prob. 5 ans.) ÷ Prob. 4 ans. = 1

(_____ ÷ _____) ÷ _____ = 1

9. Prob. 3 ans. ÷ (Prob. 5 ans. ÷ Prob. 4 ans.) = 4

_____ ÷ (_____ ÷ _____) = 4

Create Your Own

You may use the flowchart below or create one of your own. Use the rectangles as instruction boxes and the diamonds as decision boxes. Then choose a partner, exchange flowcharts, and check each other's work.

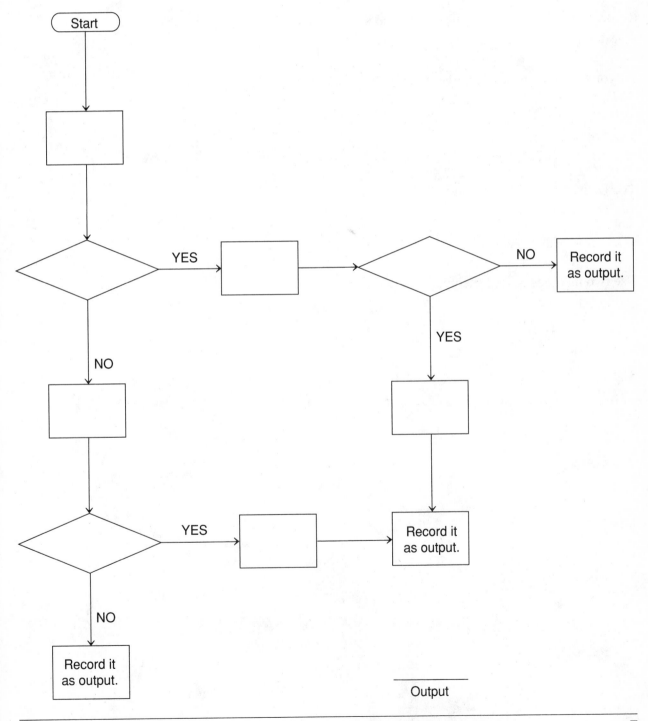

Output _____

Investigating the Distributive Property

Explore

Examine the rectangle to the right.

Analyze

To determine its perimeter, the sum of the length of its sides, you could write:

$P = (2 \times 8 \text{ m}) + (2 \times 3 \text{ m}) = 22 \text{ m}$

Or you could devise the following method:

$P = 2 \times (8 \text{ m} + 3 \text{ m}) = 22 \text{ m}$

8 m
3 m   3 m
8 m

Generalize

$(2 \times \underline{\hspace{1cm}}) + (2 \times \underline{\hspace{1cm}}) = 2 \times (8 + 3)$

The Distributive Property can be used to find perimeters more easily.

Verify

Use two methods to find each perimeter below.

6 cm
2 cm   2 cm
6 cm

10 cm
1 cm   1 cm
10 cm

1. $P = (2 \times \underline{\hspace{1cm}}) + (2 \times \underline{\hspace{1cm}})$

$P = 2 \times (\underline{\hspace{1cm}} + \underline{\hspace{1cm}})$

$P = \underline{\hspace{1cm}}$ cm

2. $P = (2 \times \underline{\hspace{1cm}}) + (2 \times \underline{\hspace{1cm}})$

$P = 2 \times (\underline{\hspace{1cm}} + \underline{\hspace{1cm}})$

$P = \underline{\hspace{1cm}}$ cm

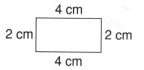

4 cm
2 cm   2 cm
4 cm

5 cm
3 cm   3 cm
5 cm

3. $P = (2 \times \underline{\hspace{1cm}}) + (2 \times \underline{\hspace{1cm}})$

$P = 2 \times (\underline{\hspace{1cm}} + \underline{\hspace{1cm}})$

$P = \underline{\hspace{1cm}}$ cm

4. $P = (2 \times \underline{\hspace{1cm}}) + (2 \times \underline{\hspace{1cm}})$

$P = 2 \times (\underline{\hspace{1cm}} + \underline{\hspace{1cm}})$

$P = \underline{\hspace{1cm}}$ cm

Digit Switch

Using compatible numbers or other mental math techniques, solve each problem below.

1. Use the digits 3, 5, and 8 once each to fill in the boxes. Obtain a product as close to 270 as possible without going over.

2. Use the digits 4, 5, and 9 twice each to fill in the boxes. Obtain a sum as close to 1,050 as possible. Obtain a difference as close to 500 as possible without going over.

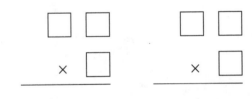

3. Use the digits 2, 5, and 7 once each to fill in the boxes. Write two problems with products as close to 140 as possible. One should be less than 140 and one should be greater than 140.

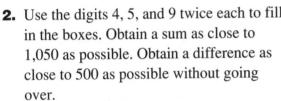

4. Use the digits 6, 7, 8, and 9 once each to fill in the boxes. The sum should be between 140 and 150.

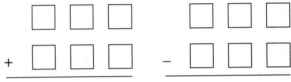

5. Use the digits 6, 7, 8, and 9 to fill in the boxes. The difference in each problem should be between 20 and 30.

Name _____

What into What?

Each number below is the estimated quotient of one number on board A divided by one number on board B. Write the correct division problem below each estimated quotient. Estimate by substituting compatible numbers or by rounding each factor.

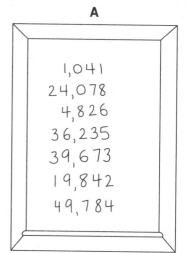

A

1,041
24,078
4,826
36,235
39,673
19,842
49,784

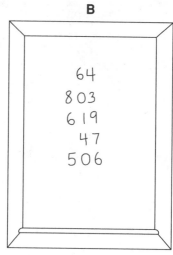

B

64
803
619
47
506

1. 60

_____

2. 2

_____

3. 100

_____

4. 80

_____

5. 30

_____

6. 400

_____

7. 10

_____

8. 600

_____

9. 40

_____

10. 20

_____

11. 50

_____

12. 1,000

_____

Name _____

Growing Up

Read each problem below. Decide which questions can be
answered with the data given. (A) Write the answers.
Where there are not enough data, tell what else you need to
know in order to answer the question. (B) Tell which
calculation method is most appropriate: mental math, paper
and pencil, or calculator.

1. If you multiply my age by 6 and add 28,
you get 100. How old am I?

(A) _____

_____

(B) _____

2. Five years from now, I will be 15 years
old. In what year was I born?

(A) _____

_____

(B) _____

3. My brother and I were born on the same
day, but I am 2 years older than he is. On
our last birthday, we each had a cake with
a number of candles equal to our age. In
all, there were 26 candles used. How old
are we?

(A) _____

_____

(B) _____

4.

| 12 plates | 25 plates | 20 plates |

You need to buy some paper plates for a
birthday party. How many of each
package should you buy to have the
fewest number of extra plates?

(A) _____

_____

(B) _____

5. Nina is older than Ted. Ted is 5 years
older than Sue Ann. What is the
difference in the ages of the oldest and the
youngest?

(A) _____

_____

(B) _____

6. Choose a friend. Which of you is older?
How many minutes older?

(A) _____

_____

(B) _____

The Flow of Algebra

Follow the steps of each flowchart.

1.

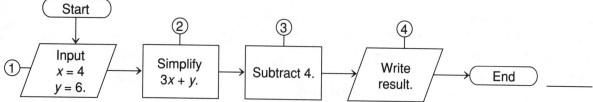

Start

① Input $x = 4$ $y = 6$. → ② Simplify $3x + y$. → ③ Subtract 4. → ④ Write result. → End _____

2.

Start

① Input $x = 7$ $y = 3$. → ② Simplify $8x - y$. → ③ Add the digits. → ④ Write result. → End _____

3.

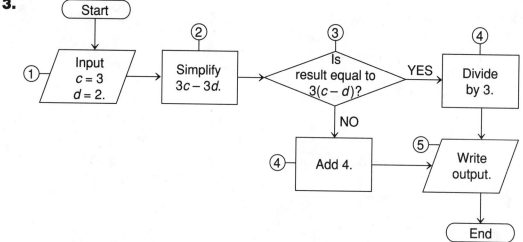

Start

① Input $c = 3$ $d = 2$. → ② Simplify $3c - 3d$. → ③ Is result equal to $3(c - d)$? —YES→ ④ Divide by 3.

NO ↓

④ Add 4. → ⑤ Write output. → End _____

4.

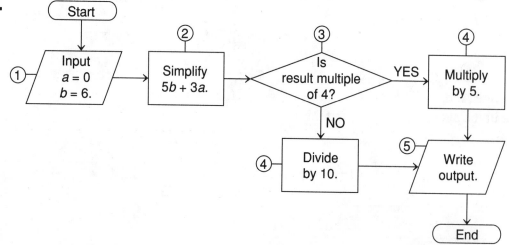

Start

① Input $a = 0$ $b = 6$. → ② Simplify $5b + 3a$. → ③ Is result multiple of 4? —YES→ ④ Multiply by 5.

NO ↓

④ Divide by 10. → ⑤ Write output. → End _____

Get to the Point

Decimals have been used for over 400 years. But they have not always been written as they are today. Here are three ways decimals used to be written.

Modern decimal: 1.536

Early decimals: 1/<u>536</u>
                  1⓪5①3②6③
                  1, 5'3"6'''

Write the modern decimal.

1. 0⓪4①9②

2. 35/<u>6206</u>

3. 0, 4'7"6'''

_____

_____

_____

4. 624/<u>42</u>

5. 41, 5'3"2'''

6. 0/<u>0062</u>

_____

_____

_____

Write the decimal in each of the three early ways.

7. 2.421

8. 0.627

9. 4.0561

_____

_____

_____

_____

_____

_____

_____

_____

_____

10. 18.739

11. 0.4382

12. 7.3956

_____

_____

_____

_____

_____

_____

_____

_____

_____

Make up two ways of your own to write decimals.
Then write two decimals using each of your ways.
Exchange with a friend. Decide which decimals your
friend has written.

13. _____ _____

14. _____ _____

What's Wrong?

Pretend that you are a math teacher. One of your students, B.
Fuddled, missed every problem on this paper. Describe the
error in each problem. Then rework the problem correctly.

1.
```
   482.4
   16.28
 +  3.729
 ─────────
  10.181
```

Error: _____

_____

2.
```
     0.9
 ×   0.8
 ───────
     1.7
```

Error: _____

_____

3.
```
   60.03
 − 27.48
 ───────
   33.65
```

Error: _____

_____

4.
```
    34.94
 + 264.2
 ────────
   6.136
```

Error: _____

_____

5.
```
      0.168
 ×    4.29
 ──────────
      1512
       336
       672
 ──────────
    7.2072
```

Error: _____

_____

_____

6.
```
      2.742
 ×   28.6
 ──────────
     16452
     21936
     5484
 ──────────
   581.9812
```

Error: _____

_____

_____

Name _____

The Most for the Money

Imagine that you have won a contest and can choose
$1,000 in stereo equipment—a turntable, a receiver, a
tape deck, and two matching speakers. Use estimation
to evaluate the price of the lowest-cost and highest-
cost systems.

Lowest cost _____   Highest cost _____

What components would you choose to come as close
to $1,000 as possible without going over it? Compare
your list with the lists of other students in your class.

_____

_____

_____

_____

_____

Name _____

It's Not the Same

Ring the one problem in each set that does not have
the same quotient as the others. Hint: You do **not**
have to find the quotients.

1. $0.006\overline{)36}$

   $0.6\overline{)360}$

   $6\overline{)3,600}$

   $60\overline{)36,000}$

2. $3,360 \div 140$

   $336 \div 14$

   $33.6 \div 1.4$

   $3.36 \div 0.014$

3. $1,240\overline{)64,480}$

   $12.4\overline{)644.8}$

   $1.24\overline{)6.448}$

   $0.0124\overline{)0.6448}$

4. $1.839 \div 0.3$

   $0.1839 \div 0.03$

   $183.9 \div 300$

   $183.9 \div 30$

5. $0.008\overline{)2.720}$

   $0.08\overline{)272}$

   $80\overline{)27,200}$

   $0.8\overline{)272}$

6. $7.2\overline{)169.92}$

   $0.72\overline{)16.992}$

   $72\overline{)1,699.2}$

   $0.072\overline{)0.16992}$

Make up two problem sets so that three of the
problems in each set have the same quotient and
one has a different quotient.

7. _____ ÷ _____

   _____ ÷ _____

   _____ ÷ _____

   _____ ÷ _____

8. $\overline{)}$

   $\overline{)}$

   $\overline{)}$

   $\overline{)}$

Name _____

News Math

Clip a newspaper article that includes numerical data.
Then complete the sections below.

Title of Article: _____

Topic: _____

Some Interesting Number Facts:

1. _____

2. _____

3. _____

4. _____

Write an interesting question using the facts above. Compute the
answer and explain how you arrived at it.

_____

_____

_____

_____

_____

_____

_____

_____

_____

Answer: _____

Oddities

Fill in the missing values. Use a calculator.

1. $25^{\square} = 625$

2. $76^{\square} = 5{,}776$

3. $125^2 =$ _____

4. $76^{\square} = 438{,}976$

5. $25^{\square} = 390{,}625$

6. _____ $^2 = 76{,}176$

7. $725^2 =$ _____

8. $76^4 =$ _____

9. $25^3 =$ _____

10. $1{,}076^2 =$ _____

Look at the last two digits of the bases and the answers in each column. What do you notice?

_____

_____

_____

Fill in these missing values.

11. $10 =$ _____ $+ 3^2 = 10^1$

12. $100 = 8^2 + 6^{\square} = 10^2$

13. $1{,}000 =$ _____ $^2 + 26^2 = 10^{\square}$

14. _____ $= 28^2 + 96^2 = 10^{\square}$

15. $100{,}000 =$ _____ $^2 + 316^2 = 10^{\square}$

16. _____ $= 352^2 + 936^2 = 10^{\square}$

Name _____

Problem Variables

Complete the table that accompanies each group of
problems. Then use the tables to answer the questions.

Kim can bike 3 miles in the time
it takes her younger sister Pam
to bike 2 miles.

Kim (K)	3	6	9	12	15	18	24	60
Pam (P)	2	4						

1. How many miles can Kim bike in the
time it takes Pam to travel 8 miles?

_____

2. Kim has chosen a 60-mile route for an
all-day bike trip. How long a route should
Pam choose for the same time period?

_____

_____

The school store sells Easyrite pens for
$0.60 each. During sales the store sells the
same pens in packages of a dozen for $6.86.
Complete the table based on the regular price.

3. How many pens can a student purchase
for $3.60?

_____

pens (p)	1	2	3	4	5	6	7	8	9	10	11	12
cost (c)	$0.60											

4. How much would 11 pens cost at the
school store?

_____

5. How much does a student save by
purchasing a dozen pens at the sale price?

_____

Rachel was 4 years old when her Aunt Donna
was 31 years old.

6. How old will Rachel be when her aunt is
4 times as old as she is?

_____

Rachel (R)	4	5	6	7	8	9	10	11	12
Aunt (A)	31	32							

How Can That Be?

Recall the repeating decimal patterns you have learned.
To produce a 1-digit number that repeats itself,
such as 0.2222222..., divide the 1-digit number by 9.

Continue the pattern.
$$0.2222222... = 2 \div 9$$
$$0.3333333... = 3 \div 9$$
$$0.4444444... = 4 \div 9$$
$$\vdots$$
$$0.9999999... = 9 \div 9$$

What do you notice? _____

_____

Analyze

$$3 \div 9 = 0.333333... = \frac{1}{3}$$

$$6 \div 9 = 0.666666... = \frac{2}{3}$$

$$9 \div 9 = 0.999999... = \frac{3}{3} = \underline{}$$

State this analysis in words.

_____

_____

_____

_____

_____

_____

_____

_____

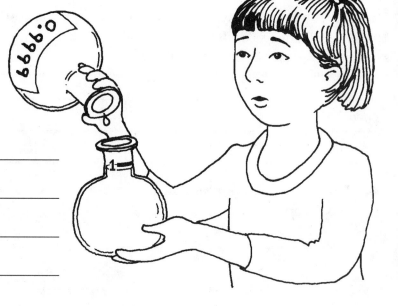

Thinking Metric

Solve.

1. One shirt button is 1 cm in diameter. How many shirt buttons placed in a line side by side would make a length 1 m long?

_____

2. A paper match is 4 cm long. How many matches placed end to end would create a line 1 m long?

_____

3. If one inchworm is 2.5 cm long, how many inchworms placed end to end would make a line 1 m long?

_____

4. One mile is 1,609.3 m long. How many kilometers equal one mile?

_____

5. One juice can is 12.5 cm high. How many cans would have to be stacked one on top of the other to create a tower 2 m high?

_____

6. One car is 4 m long. How many cars parked fender to fender would cover a distance of 1 km?

_____

7. If a $2 roll of nickels is 8 cm long, how many millimeters thick is one nickel?

_____

8. One brick is 20 cm long. How many bricks placed end to end would cover a 3-m length?

_____

9. A stack of books is 2.55 m high. If each book is 3 cm thick, how many books are in the stack?

_____

10. A freight train is 3 km long and is made up of 250 cars. How many meters long is each car?

_____

Close Enough?

Each problem below gives two measurements for the
same object. Compare the measurements. If one is
more precise than the other, write it in the More Precise
Measurement column. If the two measurements are
equally precise, put a check in the Equally Precise
column.

Measurements		More Precise Measurement	Equally Precise
1. 7,874 cm	78.7 m	_____	_____
2. 1.016 dm	10 cm	_____	_____
3. 30 m	2.88 dam	_____	_____
4. 128.75 hm	12.875 km	_____	_____
5. 59 mm	6 cm	_____	_____
6. 1,528.9 m	1.5289 km	_____	_____
7. 229 cm	22.86 dm	_____	_____
8. 73.1 mm	7 cm	_____	_____
9. 22.86 m	2.3 dam	_____	_____
10. 12,000 hm	1,200 km	_____	_____
11. 53 mm	5.2817 cm	_____	_____
12. 331.42 cm	33.1 dm	_____	_____
13. 581 hm	58 km	_____	_____
14. 22,966 m	22.966 km	_____	_____
15. 1,866 m	1.8 km	_____	_____

Measure for Measure

Complete with kL, L, mL, kg, g, or mg.

1. 0.053 kL = 53 _____

2. 0.08 kL = 80,000 _____

3. 2.2 kg = 2,200,000 _____

4. 64.27 L = 0.6427 _____

5. 34.19 g = 0.3419 _____

6. 134.78 mg = 0.13478 _____

7. 113.4 mL = 0.1134 _____

8. 100 mL = 0.1 _____

9. 0.9072 g = 907.2 _____

10. 1,338 mg = 1.338 _____

11. 5.516 L = 5,516 _____

12. 845.52 kg = 845,520 _____

13. 49.604 kg = 49,604 _____

14. 1,201 L = 1.201 _____

15. 104.72 mL = 0.10472 _____

16. 19.26 g = 0.01926 _____

17. April bought 56 _____ of gas for her car.

18. A jar of peanut butter weighs 510 _____.

19. The bottle of eye drops contained 10 _____.

20. Amanda needed 7.57 _____ of paint.

21. The Wright brothers' airplane weighed 340 _____.

22. Sam bought a bottle of fruit juice containing 1.42 _____.

23. Mrs. Smith weighs 58 _____.

24. The bottle of cough medicine holds 74 _____.

25. A blue whale weighs 136,000 _____.

26. Each headache tablet weighs 500 _____.

27. The hot water tank holds 150 _____ of water.

Is There a Problem Here?

The pictures below were used to solve
4 problems, but the problems are missing. Write
a problem for each picture. Solve your problem.

1.

_____

_____

_____

_____

_____

_____

Answer: _____

2.

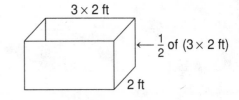

3×2 ft

$\leftarrow \frac{1}{2}$ of $(3 \times 2$ ft$)$

2 ft

_____

_____

_____

_____

_____

Answer: _____

3.

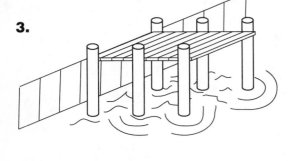

_____

_____

_____

_____

Answer: _____

4.

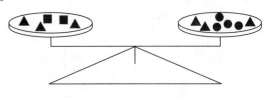

_____

_____

_____

_____

Answer: _____

Name _____

Cold Facts

Analyze the graph to answer the questions.

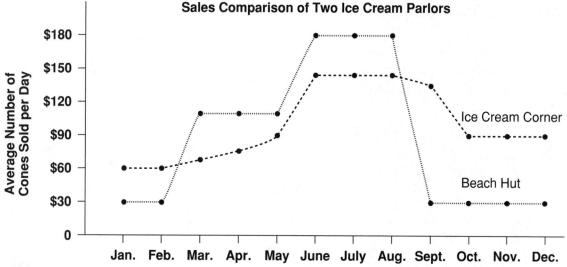

Sales Comparison of Two Ice Cream Parlors

1. Why do you think the Ice Cream Corner sold more cones in January than did the Beach Hut?

   _____

   _____

   _____

2. Why do you think sales for both businesses increased in June?

   _____

   _____

   _____

3. What was the general sales trend for both businesses in June?

   _____

   _____

   _____

4. Why do you think the Ice Cream Corner had less of a decrease in sales in September than did the Beach Hut?

   _____

   _____

5. Do you think that changes in weather conditions next year will affect the general sales trends shown here? Why or why not?

   _____

   _____

   _____

6. How might a business benefit from graphing sales figures annually?

   _____

   _____

   _____

Running in Circles

The school track team's proposed budget is due today,
but the treasurer ran out for a moment and has not
completed it. You can take over by creating categories
you think should be included in the budget. Write each
of your categories beside an appropriate percentage,
then label and title the graph below.

Category	Examples	Percent of Budget
Uniforms	25 jerseys, gymshorts, warm-up suits	30%
		24%
		19%
		15%
		7%
		_____ %

Title: _____

_____

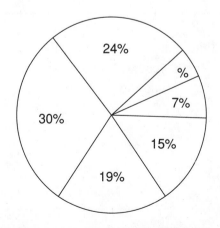

Name _____

Scattergrades

> Dear Family,
>   Our class has been studying graphing. To generate accurate data in order to complete the graph below (called a scattergram), please help your teenager keep track of the number of minutes spent on homework and studying for each school subject this week. This information will be compared with a weekly average of any scores received in these subjects. Use separate sheets to keep track of scores for each subject.

Number of Minutes Spent Daily on School Studies

SUBJECTS:					
Monday					
Tuesday					
Wednesday					
Thursday					
Friday					
Saturday					
Sunday					
Totals:					

Correlation Between Homework/Studying and Weekly Class Scores

Scores

100%
90%
80%
70%
60%
50%
40%
30%
20%
10%

Number of Minutes per Week

Is there a positive correlation, negative correlation, or no correlation between the time you spent on schoolwork and your scores?

Name _____

It All Adds Up

To find sums with many addends, try this method.
Make a check (✔) as you use each number from the
original problem.

Example: $9 + 7 + 9 + 6 + 4 + 8 = ?$

(10s) ⟶ $9 + 7 = 16$ (Check off 9 and 7.)

(20s) ⟶   Since 16 is 4 from 20, take 4 from the next number, 9, leaving 5. The 4
brings 16 up to 20. Add the remaining 5. The sum is now 25. (Check 9.)

(30s) ⟶   Since 25 is 5 from 30, take 5 from the next number, 6, leaving 1.
The sum is 31. (Check 6).

(40s) ⟶ $31 + 4 = 35$. (Check 4.) Since 35 is 5 from 40, take 5 from 8, leaving 3.
The sum is 43. (Check 8.)

So, $9 + 7 + 9 + 6 + 4 + 8 = 43$.

Complete the exercises using the mental math
technique above. Check off numbers as you proceed.

1. $8 + 8 + 7 + 9 + 8 + 7 + 5 =$ _____

(10s) ⟶ $8 + 8 = 16$

(20s) ⟶   Since 16 is _____ from 20, take _____ from 7, leaving _____ .
The sum is 23.

(30s) ⟶   Since 23 is _____ from 30, take _____ from 9, leaving _____ .
The sum is _____ .

(40s) ⟶   _____ $+ 8 = 40$. $40 + 7 =$ _____ .

(50s) ⟶   Since _____ is _____ from 50, subtract _____ from 5,
leaving _____ . The sum is _____ .

2. $8 + 9 + 7 + 6 + 8 + 9 + 4 + 6 + 7 + 9 + 5 + 3 + 9 =$ _____

Bar Graphs Versus Line Graphs

The graphs below are based on identical data. One
graph is considered more appropriate than the other for
this set of data. Analyze the graphs to answer the
questions below.

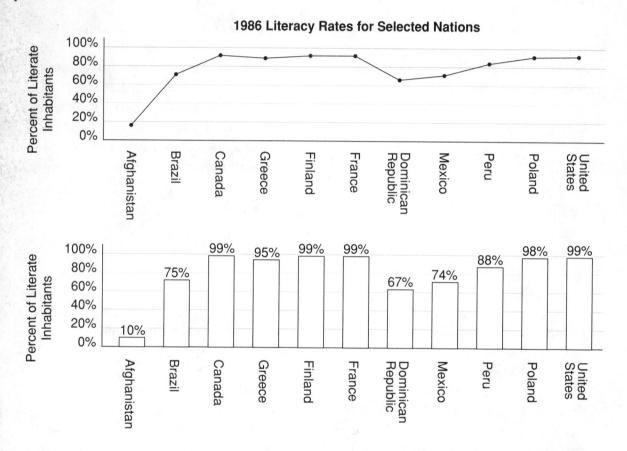

1986 Literacy Rates for Selected Nations

1. Which graph leads you to believe that the
literacy rates of the nations listed are
related and therefore reflect a trend?

_____

2. Which graph leads you to believe that the
literacy rates of the nations listed are
unrelated statistics?

_____

3. Are the literacy rates of one nation
directly related to those of other nations?

_____

4. Which graph do you feel is more
appropriate for the data? Why?

_____

_____

Name _____

Picture This

One effective problem solving strategy is to draw a picture.
Analyze each problem. Choose the letter of the picture at the
bottom of the page that relates to each problem. Then write the
answer.

1. Anne arranged her 21 glass bells so that
there was 1 less bell in each row than in
the row below it. How many bells were in
the next to last row?

Picture: _____

Answer: _____

2. A flag corp group of 21 members was in 6
rows on a field so that there was 1 less
member in the first row than in the second
row. All the odd-numbered rows had an
equal number of members. All the even-
numbered rows had an equal number of
members. How many members were in
the fifth row?

Picture: _____

Answer: _____

3. 21 centerpieces were placed on 6 tables so
that there was a total of 15 centerpieces
on the first 3 tables. The first two tables
each had one less centerpiece than the
table behind it. The rest of the centerpieces were divided equally among the
remaining tables. How many were on the
fourth table?

Picture: _____

Answer: _____

4. 21 coins were arranged in a case so that
the first two rows each had one less coin
than the row below. The last 3 rows held a
total of 15 coins in rows with equal
numbers of coins. If there were 6 rows,
how many coins were in the fourth row?

Picture: _____

Answer: _____

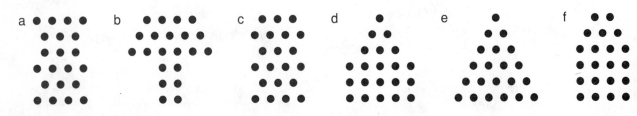

Name _____

Changing Statistics

Brian and Ella are members of an astronomy
club. The club members surveyed institutions
in their area that own large refracting
telescopes. They compiled their data in this
table. They found the mean and median of this
data. These are called measures of central
tendency. As new telescopes are perfected and
others become obsolete, the data will change.
The mean and median may also change.
Answer the questions below to discover how
these changes will affect the club's statistical
findings.

1. Find the median diameter from the data.

_____

2. Use a calculator to find the mean of the data. Round
to the nearest whole number.

Remember there are 15 telescopes. _____

Next year all the 26-inch diameter telescopes will
be sold. Two telescopes with 38-inch diameters will
be bought to replace them. Answer the questions
below using this new information.

3. Predict the median of this new set of data.

_____

Find the median. _____ What is the difference

between your prediction and the actual answer?

_____

4. Predict the mean of this new set of data. _____

Find the mean to the nearest whole number. _____
What is the difference between your prediction and

the actual answer? _____

Summer Leaves

The following data show the summer earnings of
selected 17-year-olds with jobs. Make a stem-and-leaf
table of the data and answer the questions below.

Earnings: $280, $220, $275, $275, $290, $325,
$375, $350, $325, $325, $455, $510

Stem	Leaf

1. How many students earned more than $400? _____

2. How many students earned less than $300? _____

3. What was the least amount earned? _____

4. What is the range of the earnings? _____

5. What is the mode for this set of data? _____

6. Arrange the data in order from least to greatest.

_____

_____

7. What is the median? _____

8. What is the mean? Use your calculator. _____

9. The mean and median are called **measures of central tendency**.
Why do you think they are given this name?

_____

_____

Tune to the Right Frequency

Count the number of letters in each word in the 22
word sentence that follows. Complete the frequency
table below.

> An executive with the local radio station
> has announced that an album will be
> given to each of the first fifty callers.

Number of Letters	Tally	Frequency
2	ℕ	5
3		
4		
5		
6		
7		
8		
9		

On notebook paper, write three sentences describing
the different ways that you entertain yourself in
the car on a long trip. Construct a frequency table
similar to the one above.

1. Which word length is most frequent in your

written statement? _____ letters.

Second most frequent? _____ letters.

2. How does this compare with the first table you
completed?

_____

3. Can you make any preliminary predictions based on
these tables?

_____

More Variations on Variables

Examine and complete the tables below. Write a rule in equation form that describes the relationship between the top number and the number below it.

Example:

In the table below, to find the number in the bottom row, multiply the top number by 2 and subtract 1. Since d represents the numbers in the bottom row and c represents the numbers in the top row, then $d = (2 \times c) - 1$.

c	3	5	8	12	15	18	20	30
d	5	9	15	23	29	35	39	59

Equation: $d = (2 \times c) - 1$

1.

p	2	5	6	7	8	10	13	17
q	8	20	24			40		

Equation: _____

2.

t	3	4	6	7	8	10	11	12
u	9		36					144

Equation: _____

3.

v	2	8	11	14	18	22	27	30
w	1		$5\frac{1}{2}$			11		

Equation: _____

Name _____

Get to the Point

The Camping Club has tents and sleeping bags but wants to buy additional equipment. The members asked Joe to gather information and prices so they could make wise purchases. Help the club members by reading Joe's lengthy report and completing the questions. Use a calculator.

A 2-burner camp stove retails for $34.98. A 2-gallon water jug costs $2.67. A compact double-mantle lantern costs $25.98; $12.88 will buy a floating lantern that operates on a 6-volt battery and has 12-mile visibility; a lantern with only one half the visibility sells for $9.99. A dry chemical fire extinguisher can be bought for $9.97. A warning light that can double as a spotlight or a flashlight is on sale for $7.99; a standard flashlight costs $1.99. A q-beam super spotlight with 400,000 candlepower is on sale for $17.88. Stove and lantern fuel can be purchased for $2.89 a gallon. Six ounces of insect repellent is on sale for $1.99. A twin pack of 6-volt batteries has a purchase price of $9 but has a $5 mail-in rebate in the package. A 48-quart divided cooler is $18.47. A utility water jug with a 6-gallon capacity and spout is $8.88. A 26-quart-capacity cooler can be purchased for $13.50.

1. What is the price of a double-mantle lantern and 2 gallons of fuel?

_____

2. Compute the total price of 3 coolers with 48-quart capacity and 1 cooler with 26-quart capacity.

_____

3. Which is the better buy, the 6-gallon utility jug or three 2-gallon water jugs?

_____

4. How much will it cost to buy a warning light and 15 standard flashlights?

_____

5. What is the total price of a floating lantern with 6-mile visibility and a twin pack of 6-volt batteries (after rebate)?

_____

6. If the club has 18 members and they need 1 bottle of insect repellent for every 3 people, how much will the insect repellent cost?

_____

In Perspective

Three-dimensional figures are drawn in perspective to distinguish them from plane figures. Dotted lines are used to show the edges that are hidden from view.

Use a ruler. Redraw the figures in the space provided using dotted lines to indicate edges that are not visible.

1.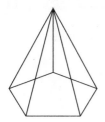

2.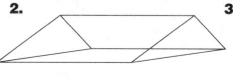

3.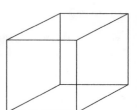

Solid figures can also be represented by patterns that can be cut out, folded, and taped.

Examine the patterns below. Circle the letter beside the patterns that could *not* be folded to form a cube.

A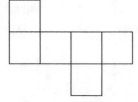

B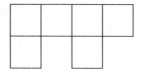

C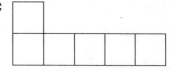

D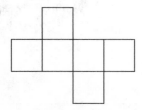

E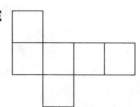

F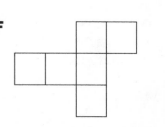

Solving Problems Mentally

Solve these problems using mental math.

1. Paco is 8 years younger than his brother who is 21. How old is Paco?

_____

2. Roseanne weighs 11 times as much as her newborn sister. Her sister weighs 9 lb. What does Roseanne weigh?

_____

3. This week Jacob received 3 times as many phone calls as his father. His father received 7 phone calls. How many phone calls did Jacob receive?

_____

4. One third of Mrs. Bergen's grocery bill was spent on food for her son's birthday party. She spent $33 on the party. What was her total grocery bill?

_____

5. One Thursday, the temperature varied 18°C in Denver. If Denver had a high temperature that day of 30°C, what was the low temperature for the day?

_____

6. Kansas became a state 65 years after Tennessee. Tennessee became a state in 1796. In what year did Kansas become a state?

_____

7. Rounded to the nearest thousand, Peru has an area that is 186,000 km² larger than the area of Bolivia. Bolivia's area is 1,099,000 km². What is the area of Peru?

_____

8. Mona Movie-Star paid 50 times more for her house than Mary Meager-Mortgage. Mona spent $2,500,000 for her house. What did Mary spend?

_____

Similar Triangles

Use a protractor and a centimeter ruler. Draw a triangle
as directed below using segment *AB*.

Step 1: Draw a 45° angle at Point *A*.
Step 2: Draw an 80° angle at Point *B*.
Step 3: The segments you drew should intersect to form a
triangle. Label the point of intersection *C*.

$A \overline{ 3\text{ cm} } B$

1. Find the length of segment *AC* in

centimeters. _____

2. Find the length of segment *BC* in

centimeters. _____

Draw a triangle as directed below using segment *DE*.

Step 1: Draw a 45° angle at Point *D*.
Step 2: Draw an 80° angle at Point *E*.
Step 3: The segments you drew should intersect to form a
triangle. Label the point of intersection *F*.

$D \overline{ 4\text{ cm} } E$

3. Find the length of segment *DF* in

centimeters. _____

4. Find the length of segment *EF* in

centimeters. _____

5. Is triangle *ABC* congruent to triangle *DEF*? _____

Why? _____

_____

6. Describe a relationship between triangles *ABC* and *DEF*.

_____

_____

Always, Never, or Sometimes?

Analyze and complete each statement below using the
word **always**, **never**, or **sometimes**.

1. An equilateral triangle is _____
an isosceles triangle.

2. A scalene triangle is _____ an
isosceles triangle.

3. An acute triangle is _____ an
isosceles triangle.

4. An obtuse triangle is _____ an
isosceles triangle.

5. A right triangle is _____ an
isosceles triangle.

6. An isosceles triangle is _____
an acute triangle.

7. An isosceles triangle is _____
an obtuse triangle.

8. An isosceles triangle is _____
a right triangle.

9. An acute triangle is_____ an
equilateral triangle.

10. An equilateral triangle is _____
an acute triangle.

11. An obtuse triangle is _____ an
equilateral triangle.

12. An equilateral triangle is _____
an obtuse triangle.

13. A scalene triangle is _____ an
acute triangle.

14. A right triangle is _____ a
scalene triangle.

15. A scalene triangle is _____ a
right triangle.

16. A right triangle is _____ an
equilateral triangle.

Parallel Segments and Angles

You will need a ruler and a protractor. Below are pairs
of parallel segments. Draw segments to form
quadrilaterals. Then answer the questions.

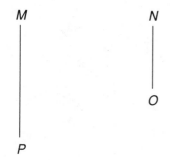

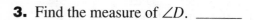

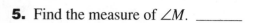

1. You may need to extend the sides of the
figures in order to measure accurately.

Find the measure of B. _____

The measure of ∠C. _____

2. Find the sum of the measures of ∠B and

∠C. _____

3. Find the measure of ∠D. _____

The measure of ∠A _____

4. Find the sum of the measures of ∠D and

∠A. _____

5. Find the measure of ∠M. _____

The measure of ∠N. _____

6. Find the sum of the measures of ∠M and

∠N. _____

7. Find the measure of ∠O _____

The measure of ∠P. _____

8. Find the sum of the measures of ∠O and

∠P. _____

9. What is unique about the sum of the measures of these

angles? _____

11. The sum of the measures of which 2 angles of a
quadrilateral with parallel sides always equal 180°?

_____

_____

_____

Balancing

Make an equation by supplying the missing numbers.

1. $(8 - \boxed{}) \times 4 - 1 = 18 - 5 + \boxed{}$

2. $12 + \boxed{} + 6 - 5 = 78 \div \boxed{}$

3. $(10 \div \boxed{}) + 6 \times 3 = (12 \div \boxed{}) \times 6$

4. $144 \div (\boxed{} \times 2) = 24 - \boxed{}$

5. $(7 \times \boxed{}) - 7 = (8 \times \boxed{}) + 2$

6. $17 - (\boxed{} \times 2) = \boxed{} \div 3$

Follow the directions. Decide if the resulting expression is an equation. Write **yes** or **no** and tell why.

7. $48 - 4 = 44$
Add 6 to each side.

_____

_____

8. $(11 - 5) \times 2 = 7$
Add 5 to the right side.

_____

_____

9. $[(39 \div 3) + 5] \div 3 = 6$
Subtract 6 from the left side.

_____

_____

10. $(14 + 8 - 6) - 2$
Add 4.

_____

_____

11. $6 > 3.5 + 1.5$
Change > to =.

_____

_____

12. $360 \div 5 = 72 + 1$
Subtract 1 from each side.

_____

_____

Two Unknowns

Equations are often used to solve problems. Read each problem and examine the equations below it. Use Guess and Check to find a pair of numbers from the variable box that makes both equations true. Write the numbers in the spaces provided. Each pair of variables is used only once.

```
┌─────────────────────────────────────────────┐
│            Values for Variables             │
│   a = 3 and b = 2     a = 4 and b = 6       │
│   a = 2 and b = 5     a = 2 and b = 4       │
└─────────────────────────────────────────────┘
```

1. 26 science students formed 6 study groups made up of 4 or 5 members each. How many groups had 5 members? 4 members?

Let a stand for the number of groups with 5 members; let b stand for the number of groups with 4 members.

$$a + b = 6$$
$$(a \times 5) + (b \times 4) = 26$$

$a =$ _____ $b =$ _____

2. 38 cheerleaders formed 10 groups of 3 or 5 to practice "human pyramids" at cheerleading camp. How many groups have 5 cheerleaders? 3 cheerleaders?

Let a stand for the number of groups having 5 cheerleaders; let b stand for the number of groups having 3 cheerleaders.

$$a + b = 10$$
$$(5 \times a) + (3 \times b) = 38$$

$a =$ _____ $b =$ _____

3. 24 toddlers were placed in 7 play groups. Some groups had 2 toddlers; some had 4 toddlers. How many groups had 2 toddlers? 4 toddlers?

Let a stand for the number of groups having 2 toddlers; let b stand for the number of groups having 4 toddlers.

$$a + b = 7$$
$$(2 \times a) + (4 \times b) = 24$$

$a =$ _____ $b =$ _____

4. 24 student government members were organized into 5 committees of 4 or 6 students. How many committees had 4 students? 6 students?

Let a equal the number of committees with 4 students; let b equal the number of committees with 6 students.

$$a + b = 5$$
$$(4 \times a) + (6 \times b) = 24$$

$a =$ _____ $b =$ _____

Angles All Over

Look at parallel lines *a* and *b* which are cut by transversals *q* and *r*. Determine the measure of each of the numbered angles.

Given: $a \parallel b$ m∠2 = 90° m∠15 = 140°

1. m∠1 _____ m∠3 _____

    m∠4 _____ m∠9 _____

    m∠10 _____ m∠11 _____

    m∠12 _____

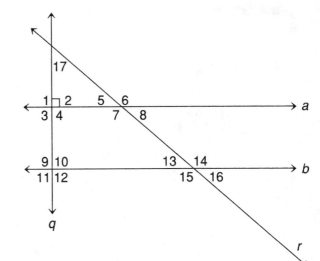

2. m∠16 _____ m∠14 _____

    m∠13 _____ m∠7 _____

    m∠8 _____ m∠6 _____

    m∠5 _____

3. m∠17 = _____

4. m∠13 + m∠17 = _____ Compare this to m∠9. _____

5. m∠10 + m∠17 = _____ Compare this to m∠14. _____

6. If m∠13 = *x* and m∠8 = *y*, write the relationship of
    x and *y* as an equation. _____

7. If m∠6 = *z* and m∠8 = *w*, write the relationship of
    z and *w* as an equation. _____

Floor Plan Fun

Dear Family,
  Our class has been learning how to construct parallel and perpendicular lines. With your teenager, examine the kitchen floor plan. Notice all of the parallel and perpendicular lines. Then, help your seventh grader draw a floor plan of a room in your home using a compass and a straightedge.

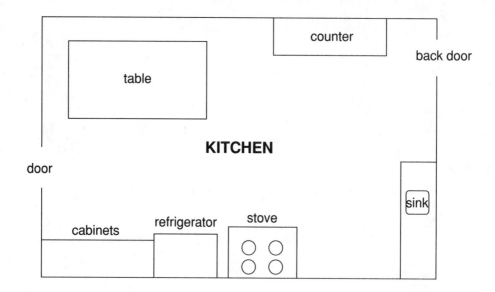

Your plan:

Baby Squares

A. Construct a perpendicular line segment running down from point *A*.

A ————————————→

B. Use your ability to "drop a perpendicular" from a point on a line in the construction that follows.

1. Find the midpoint of each side of the square. Label the midpoint of $\overline{AB}$ as *P*, the midpoint of $\overline{BC}$ as *Q*, the midpoint of $\overline{CD}$ as *R*, and the midpoint of $\overline{AD}$ as S.

2. Connect *A* to *R* and extend the line past the midpoint by about $\frac{1}{2}$ in. Follow the same procedure for *B* to *S*, *C* to *P*, and *D* to *Q*.

3. Drop perpendiculars from each corner to meet the extended lines as follows:

> *A* to $\overline{CP}$
> *B* to $\overline{DQ}$
> *C* to $\overline{AR}$
> *D* to $\overline{BS}$

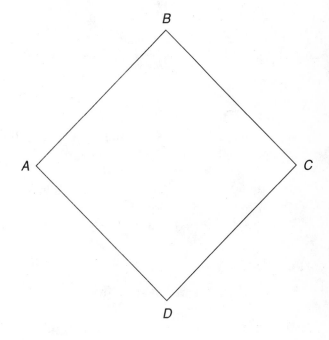

From one square, you have made five squares. Do you think that the area of the original square is more than, less than, or the same as the area of the five new squares?

_____

_____

Name _____

Triangle Trials

1. Using a compass and a ruler, try to construct a triangle
that has sides that are $\frac{1}{2}$ in., 1 in., and 3 in. long.

Look at $\triangle ABC$. Notice that when the lengths of any two sides
are added together, the sum is greater than the length of the
third side.

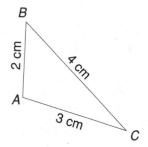

$$2 + 3 > 4$$
$$2 + 4 > 3$$
$$3 + 4 > 2$$

In order to construct **any** triangle, the sum of the
lengths of any two sides must be **greater than** the
length of the third side.

2. Why do you think this statement is true? _____

_____

3. Ring the measures of sides from which you could form a triangle.

2, 3, 3   2, 3, 6   1, 2, 3   1, 1, 1

         5, 7, 11   30, 20, 25   14, 12, 20

7, 18, 11   100, 200, 150   7, 8, 14   22, 5, 18

Grade Book Challenge

**First Quarter
Chapter Tests**

	1	2	3	4	5
Tracy					
Javier					
Rick	70				
Jodi					

Complete Mrs. Lee's grade book for the first quarter.

1. Rick scored the same number of points for each of the remaining 4 tests and totaled 390 points for the first quarter.

2. On the Chapter 3 test, Jodi scored $\frac{3}{4}$ as many points as Rick. Javier scored $\frac{7}{8}$ as many as Rick. Tracy scored half as many as Rick.

3. Tracy scored 20 points more on her Chapter 1 test than Javier did on the Chapter 3 test, but 5 points less on her Chapter 4 test than Rick did on his Chapter 1 test.

4. As you look down the column of Chapter 2 test scores, the points increase by 5 for each person.

5. Tracy totaled 30 points less than Rick did for the quarter.

6. Jodi scored the same number of points on the Chapter 1, 4, and 5 tests. She averaged exactly 77 points overall.

7. Each time Javier took a test, his score decreased by 5 points.

From the completed table you can now conclude:

8. _____ was the most consistent scorer with the highest quarterly average.

9. _____ was the most erratic scorer, with the highest score of _____ and the lowest score of _____ .

Divisibility Dilemmas

Ring all the numbers in the parentheses that would make the divisibility sentences true.

1. 4,984 is divisible by ___?___ . (2, 3, 4, 5, 6, 7, 8, 9)

   Subtract ___?___ (3, 4, 5, 6) to get a number that is divisible by 2, 3, 4, and 6.

2. 10,722 is divisible by___?___.(2, 3, 4, 5, 6, 7, 8, 9)

   Add ___?___ (3, 4, 5, 6) to get a number that is divisible by 2, 3, 4, and 6.

3. 3,333 is divisible by ___?___ . (2, 3, 4, 5, 6, 7, 8, 9)

   Subtract ___?___ (3, 4, 5, 6) to get a number that is divisible by 2, 4, and 8.

4. Are numbers that are divisible by 6 also divisible by 3 ? _____

5. Are numbers that are divisible by 8 also divisible by 4 and 2 ? _____

6. Complete this statement: If a, b, c, are positive integers,
   and if a is divisible by b
   and b is divisible by c,
   then a is divisible by _____ .

Create your own divisibility rules.
Complete the descriptions of numbers divisible by 2 or 5.

7. If a number _____ , it is divisible by 2.

8. If a number _____ , it is divisible by 5.

It's an Open and Closed Case

The Glass School has 25 windows.
One spring day 25 students decided to have some fun.
They formed a line. Then:

The first student opened every window and drew a 1 in soap on it.
The second student closed every second window and drew a 2 in soap on it.
The third student opened every third window that was closed
and closed every third window that was open and drew 3s on all third windows.
Students continued this pattern writing soap numbers, opening windows that
were closed, and closing windows that were opened.

Visualize the windows after the twenty-fifth student finished.

1. What numbers would be on the sixth window? _____

2. Would it be open or closed? _____

3. What numbers would be on the seventh window?
Would it be open or closed? _____

4. Which windows were closed only once? _____

5. Which windows are open? _____

6. What patterns do you see? _____

_____

_____

_____

Name _____

Prime Time

1	2	3	4	5	6	7	8	9	10	11	12
13	14	15	16	17	18	19	20	21	22	23	24
25	26	27	28	29	30	31	32	33	34	35	36
37	38	39	40	41	42	43	44	45	46	47	48
49	50	51	52	53	54	55	56	57	58	59	60
61	62	63	64	65	66	67	68	69	70	71	72
73	74	75	76	77	78	79	80	81	82	83	84
85	86	87	88	89	90	91	92	93	94	95	96
97	98	99	100	101	102	103	104	105	106	107	108
109	110	111	112	113	114	115	116	117	118	119	120

Follow these directions for finding the prime numbers in the box above.

▶ Cross out 1. It is not prime.

▶ 2 is a prime. Ring it. Cross out each second number after 2.

▶ 3 is prime. Ring it. Cross out each third number after 3.

▶ 5 is prime. Ring it. Cross out each fifth number after 5.

▶ 7 is prime. Ring it. Cross out each seventh number after 7.

▶ The numbers ringed or not crossed out are all the prime numbers less than 120.

1. How many primes are less than 100?

_____

2. Which number is not prime: 73, 83, 93, or 103?

_____

3. List all the composite numbers from 100 to 110 and give their prime factorizations.

_____

_____

_____

_____

Name _____

Factor Graphs and GCF

1. Complete the factor graph for numbers 9 through 24.

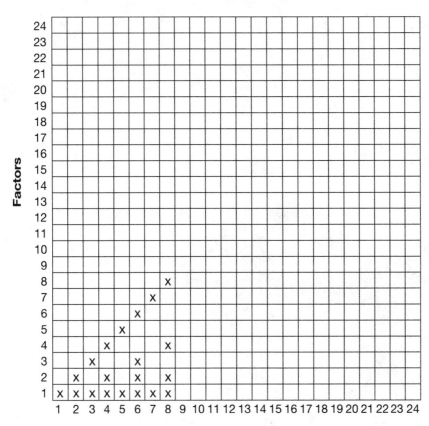

Use the factors graph to answer these questions.

2. What numbers have 2 as a factor? _____

3. What numbers have 1 as a factor? _____

4. What numbers have 4 as a factor? _____

5. What are the common factors of 8 and 12? _____

6. What is the greatest common factor of 8 and 12? _____

7. What is the greatest common factor of 8 and 10? _____

8. What is the greatest common factor of 12 and 24? _____

9. Why are there no X's above the diagonal from the lower left to the upper right? _____

_____

LCM and GCF Together

Fill in the empty boxes.

1.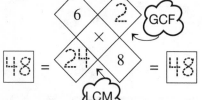

$48 = 24 \times 8 = 48$ (GCF) (LCM) with 6, 2

2.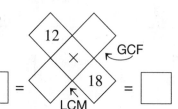

$\square = 12 \times 18 = \square$ GCF, LCM

3.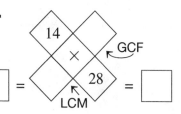

$\square = 14 \times 28 = \square$ GCF, LCM

4.

$\square = 18 \times 3 = \square$ GCF, LCM

5.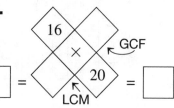

$\square = 16 \times 20 = \square$ GCF, LCM

6.

$\square = 21 \times \square = 147$ GCF, LCM

7.

$\square = 36 \times 3 = \square$ GCF, LCM

8.

$\square = 36 \times \square = 720$ GCF, LCM

9.

$\square = 16 \times \square = 96$ GCF, LCM

Draw a conclusion about two numbers and their LCM and GCF.

_____

Make three LCM and GCF charts like those above. Fill in all the boxes.

10.

$\square = \square \times \square = \square$ GCF, LCM

11.

$\square = \square \times \square = \square$ GCF, LCM

12.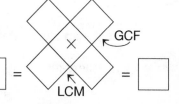

$\square = \square \times \square = \square$ GCF, LCM

Prime Discoveries

Analyze

Notice the location of the prime numbers in the following pattern.

$4 = 1 + 3$ $6 = 1 + 5$ $8 = 3 + 5$ $10 = 3 + 7$

$12 = 5 + 7$ $14 = 7 + 7$ $16 = 3 + 13$ $18 = 5 + 13$

Generalize

A mathematician named Goldbach suggested (although it has not been proven) that all even numbers larger than 2 can be expressed as the sum of two prime numbers. Test this conjecture by expressing each even number below as the sum of two prime numbers.

1. $20 =$ _____ + _____

2. $22 =$ _____ + _____

3. $24 =$ _____ + _____

4. $26 =$ _____ + _____

5. $28 =$ _____ + _____

6. $30 =$ _____ + _____

7. $50 =$ _____ + _____

8. $58 =$ _____ + _____

You can generate many primes yourself by multiplying certain whole numbers by 4 and subtracting 1 from the product. For example: Choose the number 5. Multiply it by 4 and subtract 1. The result is the prime number 19.

Create

Generate your own prime numbers using the whole numbers given below.

Example: 8 ___31___ $(4 \times 8) - 1 = 32 - 1 = 31$

9. 12 _____

10. 3 _____

11. 6 _____

12. 11 _____

13. 20 _____

14. 15 _____

What's Your Fraction Reaction?

Ring the figure whose shaded part suggests the given fraction.

1. $\frac{1}{4}$ **A**    **B**   **C**   **D**

2. $\frac{2}{3}$ **A**   **B**   **C**   **D**

3. $\frac{3}{8}$ **A** 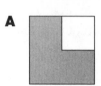   **B**   **C**   **D**

4. $\frac{1}{6}$ **A**    **B**    **C**   **D**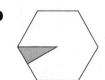

Ring the figure whose shaded part does **not** suggest the given fraction.

5. $\frac{3}{5}$ **A** 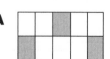   **B** 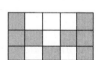   **C** 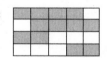   **D**

6. $\frac{1}{2}$ **A**   **B**   **C**   **D**

7. $\frac{7}{8}$ **A**   **B**   **C**   **D**

Building Lowest-Terms Fractions

Use the three given numbers to write as many fractions as you can.
Then decide which ones are in lowest terms.

1.   Fractions: _____

_____

     Lowest terms: _____

2.   Fractions: _____

_____

     Lowest terms: _____

3.   Fractions: _____

_____

     Lowest terms: _____

4.   Fractions: _____

_____

     Lowest terms: _____

Write one number in each circle. Then make your own fractions.

5.   Fractions: _____

_____

     Lowest terms: _____

6.   Fractions: _____

_____

     Lowest terms: _____

7.   Fractions: _____

_____

     Lowest terms: _____

8.   Fractions: _____

_____

     Lowest terms: _____

Mixed Patterns

Identify the pattern and fill in the missing numbers.

1. $\dfrac{1}{2}$ $\dfrac{2}{4}$ $\dfrac{3}{6}$ ☐ ☐ ☐ ☐

2. $\dfrac{2}{3}$ $\dfrac{4}{6}$ $\dfrac{6}{9}$ ☐ ☐ ☐ ☐

3. 1 $1\dfrac{1}{2}$ 2 $2\dfrac{1}{2}$ ☐ ☐ ☐

4. 1 $\dfrac{1}{4}$ $1\dfrac{1}{4}$ $1\dfrac{1}{2}$ $2\dfrac{3}{4}$ ☐ ☐

5. $\dfrac{24}{4}$ $\dfrac{20}{4}$ $\dfrac{16}{4}$ ☐ ☐ ☐ ☐

6. $2\dfrac{1}{3}$ $\dfrac{7}{3}$ $3\dfrac{1}{3}$ $\dfrac{10}{3}$ $4\dfrac{1}{3}$ ☐ ☐

7. $\dfrac{3}{2}$ $\dfrac{4}{2}$ $\dfrac{6}{2}$ $\dfrac{9}{2}$ $\dfrac{13}{2}$ ☐ ☐

8. $\dfrac{112}{8}$ $\dfrac{96}{8}$ $\dfrac{80}{8}$ ☐ ☐ ☐ ☐

Name _____

Balancing Routine

1. These scales are balanced. If the mass of the can is 30 g,
what is the mass of the book?

_____

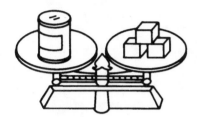  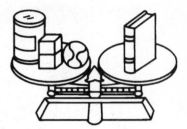

Imagine that you add 2 bags of paper clips to the left side of any scale
and 1 ball to the right side of the same scale for balance. How many bags
of paper clips are needed to equal the weight of the book?

_____

2. The stationery shop had been selling five different types of specialty
rubber bands, each type in a different-size bag — 3 oz, 5 oz, 6 oz, 8 oz,
12 oz. The manager asked Lou to combine the bags to make two variety
packs equal in weight and price. Draw bags on a scale to show how the
five bags could be balanced using one bag of each type.

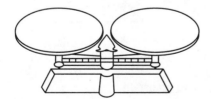

Write an equation that expresses this balance. _____

Close Decimals

Every decimal can be written as a fraction. But does every fraction have
a decimal equivalent?

Convert each fraction to a
decimal of four places.
(Do not round.)

Multiply each decimal at the left by the denominator
of the original fraction. Write your answer as a whole
number or decimal of four places. (Do not round.)

1a. $\frac{1}{8}$ = _____   **b.** _____

2a. $\frac{1}{16}$ = _____   **b.** _____

3a. $\frac{1}{10}$ = _____   **b.** _____

4a. $\frac{1}{5}$ = _____   **b.** _____

5a. $\frac{1}{25}$ = _____   **b.** _____

6a. $\frac{1}{3}$ = _____   **b.** _____

7a. $\frac{1}{9}$ = _____   **b.** _____

8a. $\frac{1}{11}$ = _____   **b.** _____

9a. $\frac{1}{27}$ = _____   **b.** _____

10a. $\frac{1}{33}$ = _____   **b.** _____

11. For a fraction and decimal to be exactly equivalent, multiplying

the decimal by the denominator should give an answer of _____ .

12. What can you conclude from the answers you found for the

multiplications above? _____

Convert each fraction to a decimal of four places. Then ring the correct label for each decimal.

13. $\frac{1}{4}$ = _____   equivalent or approximate

14. $\frac{1}{37}$ = _____   equivalent or approximate

15. $\frac{1}{99}$ = _____   equivalent or approximate

A Degree of Error

A seventh-grade math teacher put black and white sand into a jar. The teacher stated that $\frac{2}{3}$ of the sand was black. Groups of three students were to guess the total number of ounces of sand and then calculate the number of ounces of black sand. Each student in the group was to use a different form of $\frac{2}{3}$ in his or her calculation — fraction, repeating decimal to thousandths, in bar notation or decimal rounded off to thousandths.

Three friends guessed the total to be 48 ounces. (They were correct.) Each one chose a different form of $\frac{2}{3}$ to figure out the number of ounces of black sand. Calculate their answers.

Friend A (fraction): _____

Friend B (bar-notated decimal): _____

Friend C (rounded decimal): _____

1. Who had the most accurate answer? _____

2. Whose answer was the highest? _____ Why?

_____

_____

_____

3. Whose answer was the lowest? _____ Why?

_____

_____

4. The degree of error when calculating with forms of a repeating decimal is not significant here. When might the "error" in a repeating decimal become significant?

_____

_____

An Order of Fractions

Complete each fraction to make the inequality true.

1. $\dfrac{12}{19} > \dfrac{12}{\rule{1cm}{0.4pt}}$ $\qquad$ $\dfrac{5}{\rule{1cm}{0.4pt}} < \dfrac{5}{18}$ $\qquad$ $\dfrac{6}{13} < \dfrac{6}{\rule{1cm}{0.4pt}}$

$\dfrac{\rule{1cm}{0.4pt}}{17} < \dfrac{5}{17}$ $\qquad$ $\dfrac{18}{21} < \dfrac{\rule{1cm}{0.4pt}}{21}$ $\qquad$ $\dfrac{6}{23} > \dfrac{\rule{1cm}{0.4pt}}{23}$

Refer to the inequalities above and choose the best answer.

2. If a fraction has numerator of 1, as the denominator of the fraction gets larger, the fraction becomes _____ .

(smaller, larger)

3. If a fraction has a constant or unchanging denominator, as the numerator of the fraction gets larger, the fraction becomes _____ .

(smaller, larger)

4. Arrange these fractions in order from least to greatest. First use mental math or your "feel" for the relative size of each fraction to order them. Then use a calculator to be sure.

$\dfrac{10}{12}, \ \dfrac{5}{16}, \ \dfrac{8}{23}, \ \dfrac{7}{21}, \ \dfrac{3}{4}, \ \dfrac{4}{15}, \ \dfrac{5}{12}, \ \dfrac{3}{5}, \ \dfrac{7}{15}, \ \dfrac{1}{2}, \ \dfrac{9}{10}$

Order by mental math _____

Order with a calculator _____

_____

5. Give an example of fractions that could be compared easily if they had common denominators.

_____

6. Was using decimals an easier way to compare some fractions? _____

Give an example.

_____

Name _____

Unlocking Doors with Math

1. Erin remembers the three numbers 15, 22, and 33 for the combination lock on her locker, but she has forgotten the order. How many combinations of thse three numbers are possible? Use the chart to help.

1st						
2nd						
3rd						

2. Is it possible that Erin will not need to try all combinations to find the correct one?

_____

3. If Erin remembers that the first number is 22, how many combinations might she have to try?

_____

4. Joel's lock has four numbers. How many combinations are possible?

_____

5. Sandy's lock has five numbers. How many combinations are possible?

_____

6. Can you see a pattern and make a generalization about numbers required and combinations?

_____

_____

_____

Cross-Multiply Method

You can use a shortcut to add and subtract fractions.

Example: $\frac{5}{8} - \frac{1}{10} = ?$

Cross multiply the numerators and denominators. Then subtract (or add, in an addition problem).	Write that difference (or sum) as the numerator of a new fraction.	Write the product of the original denominators as the new denominator.	Write as a lowest terms fraction.

$$\begin{array}{c} 5 \quad 1 \\ \times \\ 8 \quad 10 \end{array} \longrightarrow \begin{array}{c} 50 \\ -8 \\ \hline 42 \end{array}$$

Difference (or sum) of the cross products. $\longrightarrow \dfrac{42}{80} \longleftarrow$ Product of the denominators

$\dfrac{21}{40}$

$8 \times 10 = 80$

Add or subtract using the shortcut.

1. $\frac{3}{8} + \frac{1}{6} =$ _____

2. $\frac{5}{6} - \frac{3}{4} =$ _____

3. $\frac{5}{8} - \frac{1}{3} =$ _____

4. $\frac{1}{3} + \frac{5}{9} =$ _____

5. $\frac{4}{5} + \frac{3}{4} =$ _____

6. $\frac{7}{12} - \frac{2}{5} =$ _____

7. $\frac{6}{9} - \frac{1}{2} =$ _____

8. $\frac{1}{10} + \frac{7}{12} =$ _____

9. $\frac{1}{3} + \frac{2}{5} =$ _____

10. $\frac{5}{8} + \frac{2}{3} =$ _____

11. State a formula for subtracting these fractions. $\dfrac{a}{b} - \dfrac{c}{d} = \dfrac{(a \times \quad) - (\quad \times c)}{b \times \quad}$

Name _____

A Closer Estimate

You can get a close estimate when adding and
subtracting mixed numbers by rounding each number
to the nearer half.

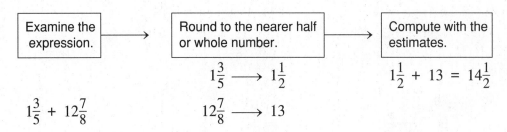

$1\frac{3}{5} + 12\frac{7}{8}$

Round these numbers to the nearer half or whole
number.

1. $\frac{21}{23}$ _____

2. $3\frac{1}{12}$ _____

3. $\frac{13}{24}$ _____

4. $5\frac{7}{15}$ _____

5. $12\frac{11}{16}$ _____

6. $9\frac{4}{5}$ _____

Use the map to the right to help you answer each
question. Estimate each answer to the nearer half or
whole number.

7. What is the distance between A City and B Burg?

_____

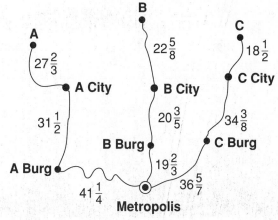

8. What is the distance to Metropolis from:

A City? _____

B City? _____

C City? _____

9. What is the length of Route C to Metropolis?

_____

Name _____

Mix It Up

Write numbers in the circles to make each problem true.

1. $7\,\dfrac{\bigcirc}{5}$

$+\,2\,\dfrac{2}{\bigcirc}$

$\overline{\quad 9\,\dfrac{3}{5}\quad}$

2. $12\,\dfrac{1}{3}$

$+\,\bigcirc\,\dfrac{\bigcirc}{\bigcirc}$

$\overline{\quad 19 \quad}$

3. $4\,\dfrac{3}{}$ $\bigcirc$ $\bigcirc$

$+\,7\,\dfrac{\bigcirc}{8}$

$\overline{\quad 12\,\dfrac{3}{8}\quad}$

4. $9\,\dfrac{2}{3}$

$+\,7\,\dfrac{\bigcirc}{6}$

$\overline{\quad \bigcirc\,\dfrac{1}{\bigcirc}\quad}$

5. $2\,\dfrac{1}{\bigcirc}$

$+\,3\,\dfrac{1}{\bigcirc}$

$\overline{\quad 5\,\dfrac{9}{\bigcirc}\quad}$

6. $\bigcirc\,\dfrac{1}{\bigcirc}$

$+\,7\,\dfrac{5}{6}$

$\overline{\quad 38\,\dfrac{23}{24}\quad}$

7. Choose one problem above and describe your "plan of attack" to find the missing numbers.

_____

_____

Write three problems, each with three missing numbers.
Exchange with a friend and solve.

8.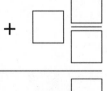

9.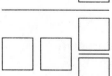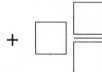

10.

Name _____

Missing Numbers

Write the missing numbers to make each problem true.

1. $18\dfrac{\square}{2}$
   $-9\dfrac{4}{\square}$
   _____
   $8\dfrac{7}{\square}$

2. $7\dfrac{7}{\square}$
   $-2\dfrac{\square}{8}$
   _____
   $\square\dfrac{23}{24}$

3. $50\dfrac{1}{\square}$
   $-\square\dfrac{3}{8}$
   _____
   $30\dfrac{\square}{24}$

4. $23\dfrac{\square}{3}$
   $-21\dfrac{\square}{3}$
   _____
   $\square\dfrac{2}{3}$

5. 18
   $-12\dfrac{\square}{4}$
   _____
   $\square\dfrac{1}{4}$

6. $\square\dfrac{5}{8}$
   $-2\dfrac{\square}{4}$
   _____
   $3\dfrac{3}{\square}$

7. Describe your plan for finding the missing numbers in Exercise 5.

How was this problem different from the rest? _____

_____

Create two of your own problems. Make sure
one of them involves renaming.

8.

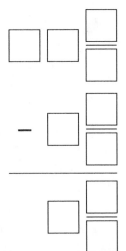

9.

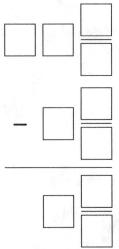

Method Switch

Solve. Draw a picture, make a table, or look for a pattern.

1. Killington Junior High School begins each day at 8 a.m. and ends at 3 p.m. If each class (including lunch) is 40 minutes long with 2 minutes in between, how many periods are there?

_____

2. Mr. Beck has a triangular garden with 7 rows. There is 1 rosebush in the first row, 3 in the second row, 5 in the third row, and so on. How many rosebushes are in Mr. Beck's garden?

_____

3. There are 8 teams in the tiny tot basketball league. Each team plays each of the other teams once. How many games will be played?

_____

4. On Monday, Bob walked $1\frac{1}{2}$ miles. Each day after Monday he walked $\frac{1}{2}$ mile more than the day before. How far did Bob walk on Saturday?

_____

5. Hector weighs 72 lb. If he gains 3 lb this year, 4 lb next year, and so on, how much will he weigh 5 years from now?

_____

6. Tanya bowled 116 in her first game. For each game after the first, Tanya bowled 6 pins more than the previous game. What did Tanya bowl for the 9th game?

_____

7. Which problems did you use a table to solve? _____

8. In which problems did you look for a pattern? _____

9. Rework one of the problems using a different method. Which method did you find easier? Why? _____

_____

Name _____

Another Way

Dear Family,
    Your seventh grader has just completed a lesson on different ways of adding and subtracting fractions. Another way of adding fractions is to convert them to decimals using a calculator, then add the decimals and convert them back to fractions. You may have used this method to calculate material requirements for projects at home.

Help your teenager follow the example and complete the exercise below.

Example:

Add $7\frac{1}{2}$ yd $+ 3\frac{1}{3}$ yd $+ 2\frac{2}{3}$ yd $+ 5\frac{1}{4}$ yd.

Round to the nearest thousandth.

a. Divide the fractions' numerators by their denominators, and write the decimals: $7.5 + 3.333 + 2.667 + 5.25$

b. Add: 18.75

c. Write the decimal as a "close" fraction: $18\frac{3}{4}$ yd

---

Add these fractions by converting to decimals.

1. $5\frac{1}{8} + 3\frac{1}{2} + 2\frac{3}{10} + 6\frac{1}{5} + 1\frac{3}{8}$

2. $6\frac{1}{4} + 2\frac{3}{8} + 1\frac{2}{5} + 4\frac{1}{10}$

_____

_____

Do you think that this process will work in the same way for subtracting fractions? _____
Give an example.

In what situations do you think that this method of adding and subtracting decimals could have problems?

_____

_____

_____

_____

_____

Pair Search

In each exercise below, use the numbers at the right to
make a set of ordered pairs so that each adds up to the
same number. Complete the function tables.

1.

x	10				
y					

$x + y =$ _____

2.

x					
y					

$x + y =$ _____

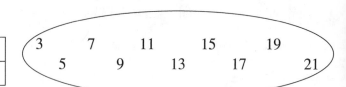

3.

x					
y					

$x + y =$ _____

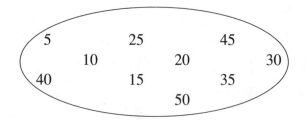

4.

x					
y					

$x + y =$ _____

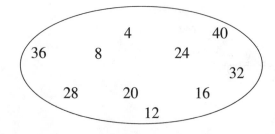

5.

x					
y					

$x + y =$ _____

Estimation and Fractions

Write a fraction in each box so that the product is
approximately ($\approx$) the one given.

Example: $\boxed{} \times 37 \approx 18$ $\left\{ \text{Estimate } \frac{1}{2}. \right\}$ $\boxed{\frac{1}{2}} \times 37 = \frac{37}{2} = 18\frac{1}{2}$

Use a fraction with a numerator of 1 in each box.

1. $\boxed{} \times 31 \approx 10$ **2.** $\boxed{} \times 23 \approx 3$ **3.** $\boxed{} \times 25 \approx 4$

4. $\boxed{} \times 111 \approx 28$ **5.** $\boxed{} \times 53 \approx 6$ **6.** $\boxed{} \times 89 \approx 18$

7. $\boxed{} \times 97 \approx 14$ **8.** $\boxed{} \times 49 \approx 4$ **9.** $\boxed{} \times 92 \approx 9$

Use a fraction with a numerator other than 1 in each box.

10. $\boxed{} \times 102 \approx 77$ **11.** $\boxed{} \times 86 \approx 57$ **12.** $\boxed{} \times 101 \approx 63$

13. $\boxed{} \times 29 \approx 24$ **14.** $\boxed{} \times 29 \approx 12$ **15.** $\boxed{} \times 57 \approx 50$

Multiplication Hexagons

Write the factors in the circles so that the product of
any three numbers along a line is the given product.
Use each factor only once.

1. Factors

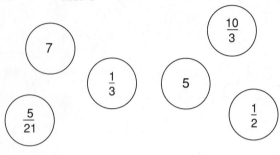

2.

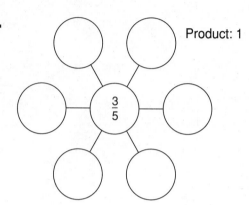

Product: 1

3. Factors

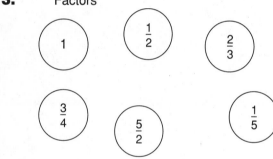

4.

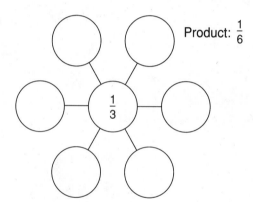

Product: $\frac{1}{6}$

5. Factors

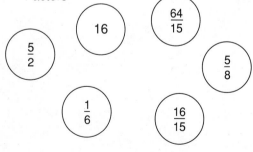

6.

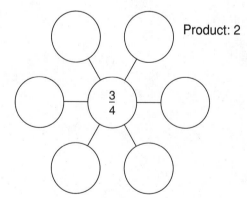

Product: 2

Name _____

Estimating Products

Carlos found a way to estimate products involving mixed numbers. Study Carlos's method.

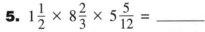

$$5\frac{1}{4} \times 2\frac{3}{4}$$

$5\frac{1}{4}$ is closer ⟶ | 5 | 3 | ⟵ $2\frac{3}{4}$ is closer
to 5 than to 6. 5×3 to 3 than to 2.

15 ⟵ Estimate

Check: $5\frac{1}{4} \times 2\frac{3}{4} = \frac{21}{4} \times \frac{11}{4} = \frac{231}{16} = 14\frac{7}{16}$

Use Carlos's method to estimate the product for each problem. Then check to find the actual product.

1. $7\frac{1}{2} \times 4\frac{1}{5} = $ _____

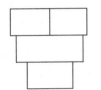

2. $8\frac{1}{4} \times 6\frac{5}{6} = $ _____

3. $12\frac{4}{9} \times 20\frac{2}{5} = $ _____

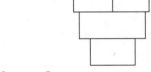

4. $3\frac{1}{3} \times 2\frac{1}{2} \times 6\frac{5}{6} = $ _____

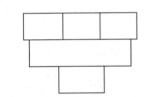

5. $1\frac{1}{2} \times 8\frac{2}{3} \times 5\frac{5}{12} = $ _____

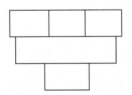

6. $4\frac{3}{4} \times 1\frac{1}{3} \times 6\frac{5}{9} = $ _____

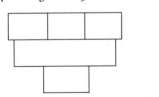

7. $6\frac{1}{5} \times 3\frac{1}{3} \times 4\frac{5}{6} = $ _____

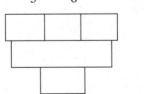

8. $10\frac{1}{5} \times 2\frac{1}{2} \times 1\frac{1}{4} = $ _____

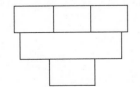

9. $9\frac{1}{3} \times 8\frac{9}{10} \times 10\frac{7}{8} = $ _____

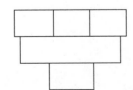

Complex Fractions

A complex fraction is a way to show the division
of two fractions.

$$\frac{\frac{3}{4}}{\frac{5}{6}}$$ is a complex fraction. It means $\frac{3}{4} \div \frac{5}{6}$.

Complex fractions can be simplified by
multiplying the numerator and denominator
by a common multiple.

Example: $\frac{\frac{3}{4}}{\frac{5}{6}} \longrightarrow \frac{\frac{3}{4} \times 12}{\frac{5}{6} \times 12} = \frac{9}{10}$

Simplify these complex fractions.

1. $\frac{\frac{9}{10}}{\frac{2}{5}} \longrightarrow$

2. $\frac{\frac{1}{2}}{\frac{1}{3}} \longrightarrow$

3. $\frac{\frac{5}{6}}{\frac{3}{4}} \longrightarrow$

4. $\frac{\frac{3}{8}}{\frac{1}{2}} \longrightarrow$

5. $\frac{\frac{7}{10}}{\frac{11}{20}} \longrightarrow$

6. $\frac{\frac{1}{4}}{\frac{6}{5}} \longrightarrow$

7. $\frac{\frac{1}{6}}{\frac{5}{9}} \longrightarrow$

8. $\frac{\frac{7}{4}}{\frac{1}{4}} \longrightarrow$

9. $\frac{\frac{4}{5}}{\frac{5}{7}} \longrightarrow$

10. $\frac{\frac{5}{8}}{\frac{1}{3}} \longrightarrow$

Name _____

Mixing It up with Division

Here is another way to divide mixed numbers.

Example:

$$2\frac{3}{4} \div 1\frac{1}{5}$$

▶ Rewrite the mixed numbers as improper fractions with a common denominator.

$$\frac{11}{4} \div \frac{6}{5} = \frac{55}{20} \div \frac{24}{20}$$

▶Divide the numerators.

$$24\overline{)55} \atop \underline{-48} \atop 7 \longrightarrow 2\frac{7}{24}$$

▶Check using the traditional method.

$$2\frac{3}{4} \div 1\frac{1}{5} = \frac{11}{4} \div \frac{6}{5} = \frac{11}{4} \times \frac{5}{6} = \frac{55}{24} = 2\frac{7}{24}$$

Solve by using the new method. Write your answers in lowest terms. Check your work using the traditional method.

1. $2\frac{7}{8} \div 1\frac{1}{4}$

_____

2. $6\frac{1}{2} \div 3\frac{2}{3}$

_____

3. $1\frac{1}{5} \div 2\frac{1}{4}$

_____

4. $1\frac{7}{8} \div 4\frac{1}{4}$

_____

5. $3\frac{2}{9} \div 1\frac{1}{3}$

_____

6. $7\frac{2}{3} \div 3\frac{1}{4}$

_____

7. $2\frac{2}{3} \div 1\frac{1}{5}$

_____

8. $5\frac{1}{6} \div 1\frac{4}{9}$

_____

Name _____

Snail Talk

Do not solve the problems. Instead, decide whether the
answer given is reasonable or not reasonable (NR).
Circle R or NR and then explain your answer.

1. Michael needed 10 snails for his science
project. He bought 25 for $10 and decided
to sell the extra snails to his friends for $1
each. How many times the price he paid
did Michael charge his friends?

Answer: $2\frac{1}{2}$ times   **R**   **NR**

_____

_____

_____

_____

2. Michael cut a carrot into uniform pieces
and timed how long it took a snail to eat
the pieces. Snail #9 took 2 minutes to eat
3 pieces. At that rate how long would it
take Snail #9 to eat 7 pieces?

Answer: 9 minutes   **R**   **NR**

_____

_____

_____

3. At 5:00, Michael left his snails to answer
a phone call. When he returned to his
room at 5:15, he discovered that several
snails had escaped. He was able to find
most of the snails and discovered that
they had traveled an average distance of
$\frac{3}{4}$ m while he was away. At that rate how
far would a snail travel in 1 hour?

Answer: 3 m   **R**   **NR**

_____

_____

_____

4. Michael wants to make a science fair
display board that is as tall as he is—5 ft.
The height limit for display boards is
366 cm. Can Michael's board be as tall as
he would like it to be?

Answer: No   **R**   **NR**

_____

_____

_____

Name _____

What Is the Question?

Formulate a question from the information in each
problem below. Write an algebraic expression for
your question. The first one has been done for you.

1. Andrew needs to save $225 to go to
summer camp. He has only *d* dollars.

How much more money does
_____

Andrew need?   225 – *d*
_____

2. Ms. Sanchez left home at 9:07. She got to
work *z* minutes later.

_____

_____

3. It takes Norma 23 minutes to get to
school. It takes Cindy only *g* minutes.

_____

_____

4. Mr. Glenn planted *t* tomato plants, *s*
squash plants, and *p* pea plants.

_____

_____

5. Gina practiced her violin for *m* minutes
on Monday, *n* minutes on Tuesday, and *p*
minutes on Wednesday.

_____

_____

6. It is 186 km from Westport to Lawrence.
It is a longer drive of *j* km from Westport
to North Beach.

_____

_____

7. Sandy had 95¢. He bought a postcard for
b¢. Then he found 10¢ on the sidewalk.

_____

_____

8. Amy arrived at the lunchroom at 12:00.
She finished lunch *l* minutes later.

_____

_____

9. The home team scored *x* points. The
visiting team had a higher score of *y*
points.

_____

_____

10. Bobby earned $45. He spent *e* dollars on a
basketball.

_____

_____

Reverse Thinking

Create a situation for each picture and algebraic expression.

1.

Record album $\dfrac{n}{4}$

_____
_____
_____
_____
_____
_____

2.

A vacation trip $756p$

_____
_____
_____
_____
_____
_____

3.

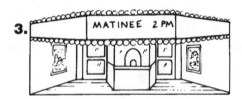

A movie theater $\dfrac{t}{8}$

_____
_____
_____
_____
_____
_____

4.

Department store sale $\$0.20s$

_____
_____
_____
_____
_____

5.

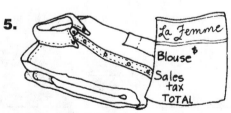

Sales tax $0.05c$

_____
_____
_____
_____

Money Matters

Write an expression for the situation in each problem.

1. Mr. McGurie bought shares in the Fast Trak Shoe Corporation for his 5 children. When the McGurie children sold the stock, they split the earnings evenly among themselves. Let x be their total earnings. Write an expression that tells how much each child earned.

2. Last year the highest price for a share of Fast Trak was $12 more than the lowest price. Let a be the lowest price. Write an expression that tells the highest price of a share of Fast Trak last year.

3. Gretchen now owns twice as many shares in Fast Trak as she bought originally. Let n be the number of shares she now owns. Write an expression that tells how many shares she originally bought.

4. Miguel has decided to invest $5,000 more this year than he did last year. Let c be the amount Miguel will invest this year. Write an expression that tells how much he invested last year.

5. The value of 1 share of Fast Trak stock decreased by $1\frac{1}{2}$ points today. Let s be the value of a share today. Write an expression that tells what the value of a share was yesterday.

6. Fast Trak now distributes shoes in 5 times more states than it did 3 years ago. Let f be the number of states 3 years ago. Write an expression that tells the number of states now.

7. Florence's earnings from her Fast Trak stock are 3 times her earnings from the interest in her savings account. Let y be the earnings from Florence's savings. Write an expression that tells how much she earns from her stock.

8. This month 18,000 more shares of Fast Trak were traded than last month. Let m be the number of shares traded last month. Write an expression that tells how many shares were traded this month.

Using a Model to Solve Equations

For each exercise, draw a model on the balance scale.
Then write an equation to solve the problem.

1. One square and one triangle balance 7
triangles. What is the weight of the square?

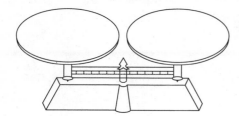

_____

2. One triangle and 2 circles balance 5
triangles. What is the weight of 1 circle?

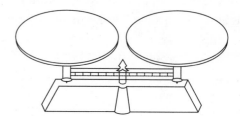

_____

3. One circle and 2 triangles balance 2
squares and 2 triangles. What is the weight
of the circle?

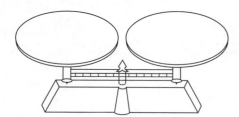

_____

4. 2 squares balance 4 circles and 4
triangles. How much does 1 square
weigh?

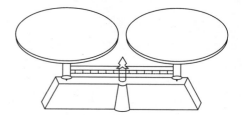

_____

5. 2 squares balance 10 triangles. Find the
weight of 1 square.

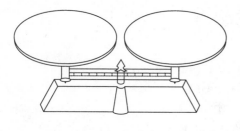

_____

6. 2 squares and 1 triangle balance 5
triangles and 4 circles. Find the weight of
1 square.

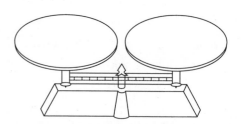

_____

_____

What Next?

In each problem below analyze the relationship
between the figures. When you have discovered the
pattern, draw the missing figures.

1.

2.

3.

4.

5.

6.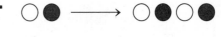

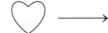

Solving Equations Using Mental Math

Write a number in each box so that the equation is correct. Use mental math.

1. $\boxed{} + t = 6,\ t = 4$

2. $\boxed{} - y = 14,\ y = 7$

3. $\dfrac{a}{\boxed{}} = 25,\ a = 200$

4. $\boxed{} \times r = 0,\ r = 12$

5. $s - \boxed{} = 12,\ s = 20$

6. $\boxed{} + m = 15,\ m = 0$

7. $\boxed{} \times n = 63,\ n = 21$

8. $\dfrac{z}{\boxed{}} = 7,\ z = 84$

Use the equations to find the missing values in each table.

9. $m + n = 15$

m	5			12	8
n		4	6		

10. $r - s = 3$

r	7	12			
s			1	5	0

11. $z \times w = 36$

z	4	6			18
w			4	12	

12. $\dfrac{a}{b} = 8$

a				56	96
b	2	4	8		

Name _____

Choose and Guess

Ring the equation that will solve the problem. Use
Guess and Check to find the answer.

1. When a certain number is multiplied by
12, the product is 120. What is the
number? Let s = the number.

$12 + s = 120$ $s - 12 = 120$

$12s = 120$ $120s = 12$

_____

2. The sum of a certain number and 18 is 59.
What is the number? Let n = the number.

$n + 18 = 59$ $18n = 59$

$n + 59 = 18$ $59 - n = 18$

_____

3. When a certain number is divided by 8,
the quotient is 13. What is the number?
Let m = the number.

$8m = 13$ $8 + m = 13$

$\dfrac{13}{m} = 8$ $\dfrac{m}{8} = 13$

_____

4. If 41 is subtracted from a certain number,
the difference is 16. What is the number?
Let x = the number.

$41 - x = 16$ $x - 41 = 16$

$x + 41 = 16$ $41x = 16$

_____

5. Wendy bought a $40 dress and a shirt.
She spent $65 altogether How much was
the shirt? Let c = the cost of the shirt.

$65 + 40 = c$ $c - 65 = 40$

$c + 40 = 65$ $40c = 65$

_____

6. Bill earns $6 an hour. If he earned $126,
how many hours did he work? Let w = the
number of hours.

$6w = 126$ $\dfrac{w}{6} = 126$

$\dfrac{6}{w} = 126$ $6 + w = 126$

_____

7. Elmer bought 4 pens for $1.96. What was
the cost of each pen? Let p = the cost of
each pen.

$\dfrac{p}{196} = 4$ $196 - 4 = p$

$4p = 196$ $196p = 4$

_____

8. 9 boxes each have an equal number of
cans in them. If there are 180 cans
altogether, how many are in each box?
Let v = the number of cans in each box.

$9v = 180$ $180 - v = 9$

$180 - 9 = v$ $180 + v = 9$

_____

Name _____

Simplify

Simplify each expression. Then give the inverse
operation that gets the variable alone.

	Simplified Expression	Inverse Operation

1. $x + (5 \times 5) + \frac{100}{20}$ _____   _____

2. $(x - 1\frac{1}{2}) + 5$ _____   _____

3. $(y + \frac{18}{3}) - 32$ _____   _____

4. $(b + 4) - (6 \times 9)$ _____   _____

5. $(c - 9) + (7 \times 2)$ _____   _____

6. $(x + 28) - (5 \times 6)$ _____   _____

7. $(y - 1) + (5 \div 2)$ _____   _____

8. $(b - 10.75) + (4 \times 5)$ _____   _____

9. $(c + 25) + (18 - 3)$ _____   _____

10. $(x - 38) - 2$ _____   _____

11. $(y + 50) - (100 \div 10)$ _____   _____

12. $(b - 12) - 6$ _____   _____

13. $(c + 36) + (100 - 64)$ _____   _____

14. $(x - 18) + 10$ _____   _____

15. $(y - 2) - (2 \times 8)$ _____   _____

16. $(b + 58) + (7 \times 6)$ _____   _____

17. $(c - 29) + 1$ _____   _____

18. $(x - 33) + (9 \times 3)$ _____   _____

Name _____

Figure It Out!

Each problem below is followed by 2 equations. Ring the equation that fits the situation. Then solve it using inverse operations.

1. Claudia had $300 left in her savings account after she withdrew $48 to buy running shoes. How much did Claudia have in her savings account before she purchased the shoes?

$x - 48 = 300$ $\qquad\qquad$ $x + 48 = 300$

_____

_____

2. Casey's language arts teacher requires 6 book reports the first semester. Casey has 4 more reports to complete. How many book reports has Casey already finished?

$x - 4 = 6$ $\qquad\qquad$ $x + 4 = 6$

_____

_____

3. Terri had a total of 12 tennis balls after she bought a can of 3 balls. How many tennis balls did she have before buying the new ones?

$x - 3 = 12$ $\qquad\qquad$ $x + 3 = 12$

_____

_____

4. Tait finds lost golf balls and sells them. After selling 13, she had 22 balls left. How many golf balls did Tait have before selling the 13?

$x - 13 = 22$ $\qquad\qquad$ $x + 13 = 22$

_____

_____

5. When Corry successfully launched his model rocket twice on Saturday, he reached his goal of 5 successful launches with one rocket. How many times had Corry launched that rocket successfully before Saturday?

$x - 2 = 5$ $\qquad\qquad$ $x + 2 = 5$

_____

_____

6. Mr. Young displayed 16 of the science fair projects in the library. He put the rest of the projects in the auditorium. Altogether there were 36 projects. How many were in the auditorium?

$x - 16 = 36$ $\qquad\qquad$ $x + 16 = 36$

_____

_____

Hi Ho, the Dairy-O, the Variable Stands Alone

Give the inverse operation that will get the variable alone.

1. $15v$ _____ **2.** $\dfrac{v}{15}$ _____

3. $w \div 138$ _____ **4.** $138w$ _____

5. $x + 6{,}901$ _____ **6.** $x - 6{,}901$ _____

7. $\dfrac{1}{9}b$ _____ **8.** $9b$ _____

9. $1\dfrac{1}{5}k$ _____ **10.** $k \div 1\dfrac{1}{5}$ _____

11. $2{,}000a$ _____ **12.** $\dfrac{a}{2000}$ _____

13. $c + 1.75$ _____ **14.** $c - 1.75$ _____

15. $z \div 2\dfrac{3}{4}$ _____ **16.** $2\dfrac{3}{4}z$ _____

17. $a - \dfrac{2}{3}$ _____ **18.** $a + \dfrac{2}{3}$ _____

19. $16y$ _____ **20.** $\dfrac{1}{16}y$ _____

All You Can Eat

Over the years Ted, has tried to break every eating contest record at the Bexar County Fair. To his dismay he has never succeeded. He has kept track of his own best efforts, however. Look at the Bexar County Fair eating contest records shown below. Use them in the problems to figure out Ted's personal bests.

Hot Dogs		Hamburgers		Pancakes (With Syrup)	Oysters	Prunes
25		21		60	300	144
	Snails		Ravioli	Peanuts		
	40 oz		5 lb	100		

1. One half the ounces of snails Ted has eaten is the same as $\frac{1}{3}$ the county hamburger record. What is Ted's personal best for snail eating?

_____

2. Five times the number of prunes Ted has eaten equals the county oyster record. What is Ted's prune record?

_____

3. Twice the number of hamburgers Ted has put away is the same as $\frac{4}{5}$ of the county hot dog record. What is the most hamburgers Ted has eaten at one sitting?

_____

4. Even though Ted adores oysters, 3 times the number he has eaten at one time equals only $\frac{1}{2}$ the county oyster record. What is Ted's personal record?

_____

5. If you halve the county peanut record you will get 2 times Ted's best pancake eating effort. What is Ted's best effort?

_____

6. Two-thirds the number of peanuts Ted has consumed is the same as the county oyster record divided by 6. What is Ted's peanut record?

_____

7. Ted has never especially liked hot dogs. Eight more than his personal best is the same as $\frac{1}{6}$ the county prune record. How many hot dogs has Ted eaten at one time?

_____

8. Three less than the number of pounds of ravioli that Ted ate is equal to 20 less than the county hamburger record. How many pounds of ravioli has Ted eaten?

_____

Ratios Everywhere

Collect the data needed to find each of the ratios
below. Hint: If one of the numbers you come up with
is a zero, substitute another number. Then write the
ratio you found in lowest terms.

1. The number of students in your room to
the number of teachers in your room

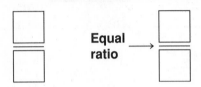

2. The number of desks in your room to the
number of chairs in your room

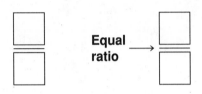

3. The number of hours your school is open
during the day to the number of hours in
the day

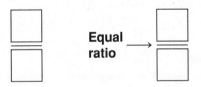

4. The number of days your school was open
last week to the number of days it was
closed last week

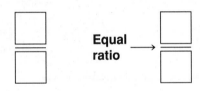

5. The number of letters in the last name of
the president to the number of letters in
the last name of the governor of your state

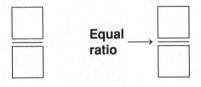

6. The number of people in your room
wearing sneakers to the number of people
in your room not wearing sneakers

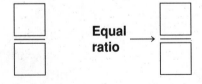

7. Were any of the ratios you wrote already

in lowest terms ? _____

How can you tell if the ratios are in

lowest terms? _____

_____

_____

8. Which ratios did you find easiest to

rewrite in lowest terms? Why? _____

_____

_____

_____

_____

Name _____

Writing Proportions

Complete to make each ratio a proportion.

1. $\dfrac{8}{5} = \dfrac{?}{20}$ _____

2. $\dfrac{24}{36} = \dfrac{?}{6}$ _____

3. $\dfrac{3}{?} = \dfrac{15}{20}$ _____

4. $\dfrac{1}{3} = \dfrac{10}{?}$ _____

5. $\dfrac{2}{?} = \dfrac{14}{21}$ _____

6. $\dfrac{32}{18} = \dfrac{?}{9}$ _____

7. $\dfrac{12}{20} = \dfrac{?}{5}$ _____

8. $\dfrac{1}{?} = \dfrac{4}{12}$ _____

9. Seventh graders were surveyed on taste preferences. 2 in 9 preferred spearmint to peppermint toothpaste. 18 preferred spearmint sugarless gum to peppermint. If the ratios for toothpaste and gum were equivalent, what is the smallest number of seventh graders that could have been surveyed for the gum?

_____

10. Explain how you found your answer to Question 9.

_____

_____

_____

Create your own proportions leaving one number missing. Exchange your paper with that of a classmate.

11.

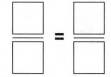

12.

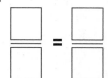

It's All to Scale

Each circle below is a scale drawing of a different type of ball used in a sport.

▶ Measure the diameter of each circle to the nearest tenth of a centimeter.
▶ Use the scale to find the actual diameter of the ball to the nearest tenth of a centimeter.
▶ Use the chart at the right to find the sport in which the ball is used.

Diameter of Balls Used in Various Sports:	
Basketball	24.0 cm
Baseball	7.5 cm
Golf	4.2 cm
Table Tennis	3.8 cm
Tennis	6.4 cm
Volleyball	21.0 cm

1.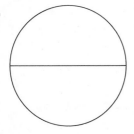

Scale:
1 cm = 2 cm

Measured
diameter: _____
Actual
diameter: _____

Sport: _____

2.

Scale:
1 cm = 10 cm

Measured
diameter: _____
Actual
diameter: _____

Sport: _____

3.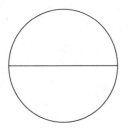

Scale:
1 cm = 1.4 cm

Measured
diameter: _____
Actual
diameter: _____

Sport: _____

4.

Scale:
full size

Measured
diameter: _____
Actual
diameter: _____

Sport: _____

5.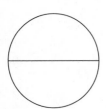

Scale:
1 cm = 3 cm

Measured
diameter: _____
Actual
diameter: _____

Sport: _____

6.

Scale:
1 cm = 15 cm

Measured
diameter: _____
Actual
diameter: _____

Sport: _____

Name _____

The Rating Game

Unit rates do not always come out evenly.

Example: If apples are 3 for $1, then $1 \div 3 = \$0.333 \ldots$

1. What price do you think a cashier at a grocery store would ring up for 1 apple in the example above? Why?

_____

_____

_____

_____

_____

_____

2. Look at Exercises 3-8. Which do you think will have an even unit rate?

_____

_____

Use a calculator to find each unit rate. Remember to round up to the nearest cent.

3. $\dfrac{\$5}{4 \text{ cards}}$

4. $\dfrac{\$10}{3 \text{ books}}$

5. $\dfrac{\$1}{4 \text{ pears}}$

6. $\dfrac{\$45.99}{2 \text{ sweaters}}$

7. $\dfrac{\$25}{5 \text{ belts}}$

8. $\dfrac{\$3}{12 \text{ cans of corn}}$

First estimate and then calculate the better buy.
Underline the better choice.

9. 1 eraser for $0.15 or 6 for $1

10. 250 tissues for $0.99 or 300 for $1.30

11. 1 pencil for $0.09 or 1 doz for $1

12. 3,000 staples for $1.25 or 5,000 for $1.98

Brain Food

Sometimes you need to estimate at the grocery store.

Estimate to find the better or best buy.

Example 1: Ground beef prices: 11 oz @ $1.99 ⎫ **Strategy: Divide each price by the**
13 oz @ $2.49 ⎬ **number of ounces to get the price**
39 oz @ $5.69 ⎭ **per ounce for each size.**

11 oz @ $1.99 At 11 oz the price is about $ _____ per ounce.

13 oz @ $2.49 At 13 oz the price is about $ _____ per ounce.

39 oz @ $5.69 At 39 oz the price is about $ _____ per ounce.
The best buy is 39 oz @ $5.69.

Example 2: Honey prices: 32 oz @ $1.56 ⎫ **Strategy: Add the missing part and**
40 oz @ $2.49 ⎬ **compare.** Bring 32 oz up to the 40-oz
⎭ level. Increase size and price by $\frac{1}{4}$.

32 oz + 8 oz = 40 oz
$1.56 + $0.40 = $1.96

40 oz @ about _____ is a _____ buy than 40 oz @ $2.49.

1. Ice Tea Mix
24 oz @ $1.89 _____

32 oz @ $1.99 _____

64 oz @ $5.99 _____

3. Straws
100 @ $0.89 _____

150 @ $1.40 _____

2. Dog Food
3 oz @ $0.25 _____

6 oz @ $0.47 _____

4. Pancake Mix
24 oz @ $1.19 _____

32 oz @ $1.29 _____

48 oz @ $1.68 _____

5. Your younger brother just bought the super-duper size box
of Videogame Cereal. He says, "This big one cost $8.99 and
the small one cost $4.79. You get more for your money with
the big sizes, so I bought the big one." (The cereals are 60 oz
and 48 oz respectively.) Give your brother some advice.

_____

_____

Name _____

The Golden Path

Look at the grid at the right and answer the following
questions.

1. The *x*-axis from 0 to 3, the *y*-axis from 0
to 5, and lines to the axes from the circled
point define a rectangle. What are its
dimensions?

_____

What is the ratio of the sides of this
rectangle?

_____

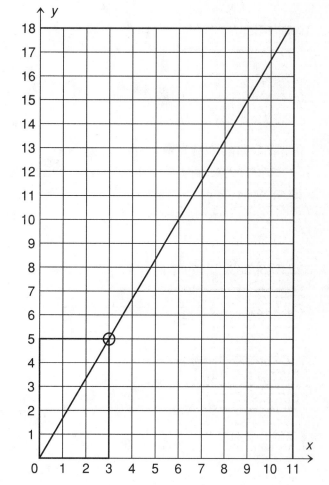

2. On this grid, through what other whole-
number vertical/horizontal intersections
does a diagonal of this rectangle pass?

_____

Draw lines from these points to the axes.
Complete the rectangles. What are the
ratios for the sides of each rectangle?

_____

3. Formulate a rule about the nature of these rectangles.

_____

_____

Name _____

Trails to Scale

The map shows different horseback riding trails.

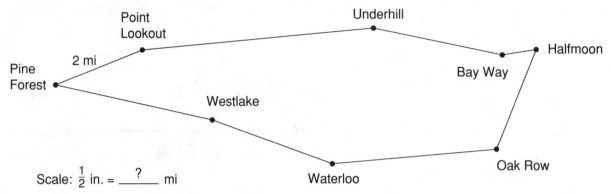

Scale: $\frac{1}{2}$ in. = ____?____ mi

1. From Pine Forest to Point Lookout is 2 miles. Use a ruler to determine the scale of the map.

_____

2. Use your scale and ruler to determine the distances along the trail.

3. Explain how you found the scale of the map.

_____

_____

_____

Make your own map below. Give it to a classmate and ask him or her to find the scale.

Name _____

Working Math

Write the rule in words, write an algebraic expression, and construct a table of values to satisfy the situations below.

Every week this summer, Aaron expects to mow 5 lawns at $9 each. Because he is using the family's mower, he has agreed to pay a "rental fee" of $2 per week. How much will Aaron have earned at the end of each week?

1. In words: _____

_____

_____

_____

2. As an algebraic expression where w = the number

of weeks: _____

3.

Weeks worked	1	2	3	4	5	6	7	8	w
Amount earned									

How would your algebraic expression in Exercise 2 change if:

4. Aaron got a raise and received $10 for 2 of his 5

lawn-mowing jobs? _____

5. Aaron gave his sister his 3 jobs paying $9 and his parents no longer charged a rental fee for the

mower? _____

Scale Drawing and Similar Figures

1. This is a sketch of the Cobbs' backyard and patio area. The measurements represent actual measurements. Assume that all angles are right angles. Write the missing measurements on the sketch, then draw the Cobbs' backyard to scale.

$$1 \text{ cm} = 1.5 \text{ m}$$

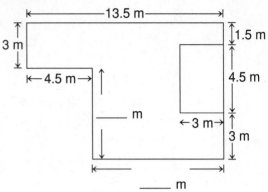

2. Write the missing measurements on this sketch of the Cobbs' front yard. Assume that all angles are right angles, then draw the yard to scale.

$$0.5 \text{ cm} = 3 \text{ m}$$

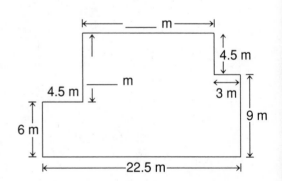

Rolling Along

Work the following problems using $\frac{22}{7}$ or 3.14 for π.

1. How many full turns will the ball make as it rolls to the bottom of the incline?

_____

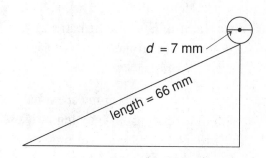

d = 7 mm

length = 66 mm

2. How many turns will the small circle make around the big circle until it returns to the arrow?

_____

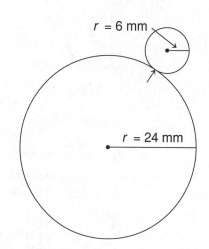

r = 6 mm

r = 24 mm

3. After she applies the brakes, the wheels on Joan's car will turn 4 times before they come to a full stop. (Assume no skidding.) Will her tire roll over the tack?

_____

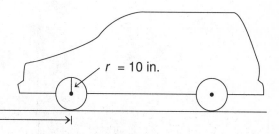

r = 10 in.

|← _____ 20 ft _____ →|

4. For one of his camp projects, Josh is using a circular stamper to design wrapping paper. The stamper and part of the sheet of paper are drawn below. If the stamper runs out of ink after 3 complete turns, how many times will Josh have to interrupt his work to reink?

_____

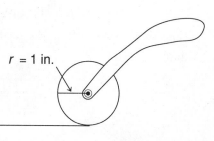

r = 1 in.

paper = 3 ft

Math Trip

Jasmine and her family went on a trip to Canada over spring break. Her math teacher asked her to tell the class about her trip in a "mathematical way." Jasmine wrote the following problems. Solve each. Use Guess and Check or Work Backward.

1. On the plane trips, Jasmine spent half as much time reading as watching movies. She wrote a letter for a hour more than the time she spent reading. She talked to her parents for $\frac{1}{2}$ an hour less than she spent writing the letter. She talked to her parents for 2 hours. How long were the movies?

_____

2. While in Canada, Jasmine's family used 3 main train lines. Each larger train line had 4 times as many trains as the next smaller line. There are 126 trains in all. How many trains does each line have?

_____

3. On Wednesday, Jasmine went to half as many shops as her mother. Her father visited 3 more than she did. Her brother visited 5 fewer than her father. Jasmine's brother went to 6 shops. How many shops did Jasmine's mother go to?

_____

4. The family spent $82 on food on Wednesday. Jasmine's mother spent 3 times as much money as her brother. Her father spent $8 less than her mother. Jasmine spent $2 more than her brother. how much did each member of her family spend?

_____

_____

_____

5. Jasmine's family bought 12 postcards. Jasmine's brother sent half as many postcards as her father. Jasmine sent 3 more than her father. Her father sent half as many as her mother. Her mother sent $\frac{1}{3}$ of the total. How many postcards did each member send?

_____

_____

6. Jasmine and her family had a great time in Canada, but they are glad to be home. The family had 9 suitcases in all. Write your own word problem that can be answered using Guess and Check or Work Backward using this information.

_____

_____

Name _____

Color by Percent

Using colored pencils, shade in the grids using the data
given, and then answer the questions.

1. 5% of the squares are green. The number of blue
squares is 5 times the number of green ones.
The number of red squares is 30 more than the
number of blue ones.

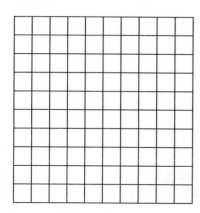

How many of the squares are green? _____

What percent of the squares are blue? _____

What percent of the squares are red? _____

What percent of the squares are not shaded? _____

2. $\frac{48}{100}$ of the squares are green. 20% of the squares
are not shaded. The number of blue squares is $\frac{1}{2}$
the number of green ones. The remaining squares
are red.

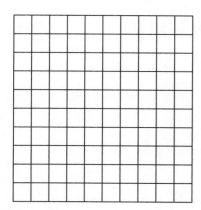

How many squares are red? _____

What percent of the squares are green? _____

How many squares are not shaded? _____

What percent of the squares are blue? _____

What fraction of the squares are blue? _____

Name _____

Party Percents

Analyze the given information to answer the questions below.

Adriana threw a party. She invited 26 girls and 36 boys from her school. She also invited 26 girls and 12 boys from her youth group. 85 of the 100 people invited were able to attend.

	Percent	Lowest-Terms Fraction for Each Percent
1. What percent of those invited were boys?	_____	_____
2. What percent of those invited were girls?	_____	_____
3. What percent were able to attend the party?	_____	_____
4. What percent were not able to attend?	_____	_____
5. What percent of those invited were from school?	_____	_____
6. What percent of those invited were from her youth group?	_____	_____

7. How many boys were invited? _____   **8.** How many girls were invited? _____

	Lowest-Terms Fraction	Percent for Each Fraction
9. What fraction of the boys invited were from school?	_____	_____
10. What fraction of the boys invited were not from school?	_____	_____
11. What fraction of the girls invited were from school?	_____	_____
12. What fraction of the girls invited were not from school?	_____	_____

What Do You Like to Do?

In a recent study, 80 high school students were polled about their favorite summer sport. Their preferences are given in the chart.

Activity	Number of Votes
swimming	32
basketball	20
volleyball	16
biking	8
tennis	4

	Percent	*Percent Expressed as a Decimal*

1. Swimming received what percent of the votes? _____ _____

2. What percent of the votes did basketball get? _____ _____

3. What percent of the students voted for volleyball? _____ _____

4. What percent of the students said that biking was their favorite summer sport? _____ _____

5. What percent of the votes did tennis get? _____ _____

TOTALS

Relate the poll results to the parts of a circle. Make a circle graph using your percentages.

Summer Sports Preferences Among 80 H.S. Students

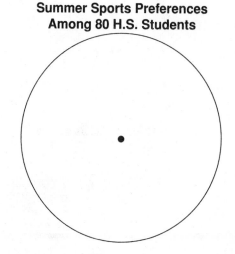

The Better Deal

Solve each problem. Explain your answer.

1. Two stores were having a sale on $48 sneakers. Store A was selling them at 30% off and Store B was selling them at $\frac{2}{5}$ off the original price. Which store was offering the better deal?

_____

_____

2. At her Saturday night waitressing job, Susan had two tables that each had a check of $72. The Johnson family left Susan a tip that was 15% of their check. The Ramirez family left Susan a tip of $11. Which family left a bigger tip?

_____

_____

3. Trung had a part-time job selling newspaper and magazine subscriptions. He earned a certain percent of each subscription that he sold. He was paid 15% of his total newspaper sales and $\frac{1}{6}$ of his total magazine sales. Did he earn a larger percent selling a newspaper subscription or a magazine subscription?

_____

_____

4. Jackets that originally sold for $30 were on sale at a department store. In the men's department the jackets were marked 20% off, and in the women's department the jackets were selling for $\frac{4}{5}$ of the original price. The sale price in both departments was $24. How is that possible?

_____

_____

_____

_____

S A L E

- *Choose the best deal!*

- *75% of original price!*

- *25% off!*

- *$\frac{1}{4}$ off*

Name _____

Figure The Function

Analyze each table to decide what the function
rule is. Complete each table and write the
function on rule

1.

x	0	1	2	5	6	8	10	13
f(x)	10	11	12	15	16	18		

f(x) = _____

2.

w	0	1	2	3	10	12	14
f(w)	14	13	12	11	4		

f(w) = _____

3.

k	0	1	2	3	4	5	10
f(k)	5	6	9	14			105

f(k) = _____

4.

j	0	1	2	3	4	5	6	7
f(j)	50	49	46	41	34			

f(j) = _____

5.

z	0	1	2	3	4	5	6	10
f(z)	3	6	9	12				33

f(z) = _____

6.

y	0	2	4	6	8	10	12	100
f(y)	3	4	5	6	7			53

f(y) = _____

Above and Below Quota

At the XYZ Company, each salesperson has a quota of 25 computers per month. With one week left to go in the month, Susan has already sold 30 computers. Trina has sold 22, but Marty has sold only 10 computers. The computer company as a whole must sell 50,000 computers each month.

1. What percentage of her quota has Susan already sold?

_____

2. If by the end of the month Susan can increase her sales by 20% of what she has already sold, what percentage of her quota will she sell?

_____

3. In order to sell 160% of his quota, how many more computers will Marty have to sell?

_____

4. If Marty does sell 160% of his quota, what percent of his 10 computer sales would this be?

_____

5. If by the end of the month Trina sells an additional 100% of what she has already sold, how many computers will she have sold in all?

_____

6. What percent of her quota would this be?

_____

7. Each person's quota is what percent of the company's quota?

_____

8. If Marty does not sell any more computers, what percent of the company's quota will he have sold?

_____

Name _____

Percents of Polygons

Each of the polygons is regular. The diagonals of each
polygon have been drawn to form triangles in order to
determine the sum of the measures of the angles.
Complete the table below by looking for patterns in
the given relationships. Round percents to the
nearest tenth.

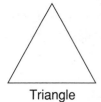
Triangle

Square

Pentagon

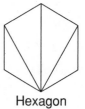
Hexagon

Number of Sides	Number of Triangles	Sum of the Angles	Each Angle of the Polygon	Percent Each Angle is of the Sum
3	1	180°	60°	33.3
4	2	360°	90°	25
5	3	540°		
6	4			
7				
8				
9				
10				

Name _____

Weather or Not

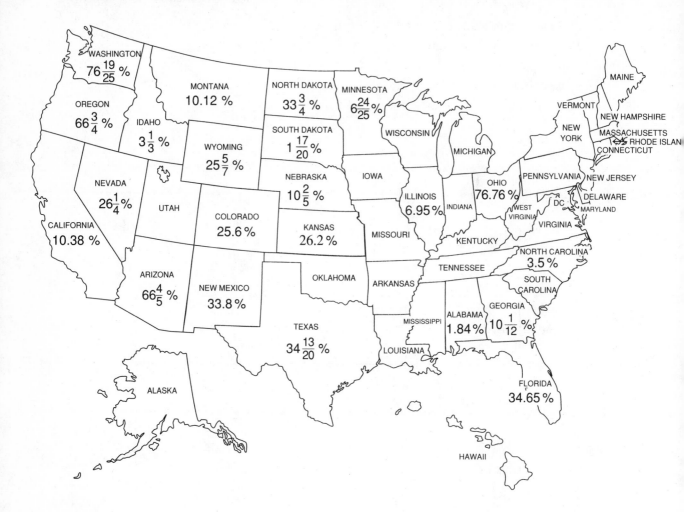

One year it rained much more than usual. The map gives the percent of increase in rainfall for some states that year. Compare the percentage increases in rainfall for each state below. In each case, circle the name of the state that had a greater percentage increase. If both states had the same percentage increase, circle both names.

New Mexico or North Dakota   Florida or Texas   Nevada or Kansas

Idaho or North Carolina   Illinois or Minnesota   Colorado or Wyoming

Montana or Georgia   Arizona or Oregon   California or Nebraska

Alabama or South Dakota   Washington or Ohio

What Is Your Color?

Sophomores at City High School were asked what
color they would like their first car to be. The results
of the survey have been compiled in the table.
Estimate the answers to the questions below.

	Red	Black	Blue	Yellow	White
Girls	19	17	10	5	2
Boys	13	24	9	2	1

1. About what percent of the sophomores questioned
   were girls?   _____

2. Estimate what percent of the girls would like a
   black car.   _____

3. Estimate what percent of the boys would like a
   blue car.   _____

4. About what percent of the girls would like either
   a blue or a black car?   _____

5. Of the people who would like a red car, about
   what percent are boys?   _____

6. Estimate what percent of the students would like
   a white car.   _____

7. About what percent of the boys would like a
   yellow car?   _____

8. About what percent of the boys would like a red
   or a black car?   _____

9. Estimate what percent of the girls would like a
   yellow car.   _____

10. Of the people who would like either a red or a
    yellow car, about what percent were girls?   _____

Solve and Compare

Solve the following problems using the Act Out or Use Objects strategies.

At a computer demonstration there are two computers, each one with a different game. Each one of the games takes three minutes to play, but you cannot play Game B until you have completed Game A.

1. How long will it take four people to play both games?   _____

2. How long will it take five people to play both games?   _____

3. How long will it take four people to play both games if it does not matter if you start with Game A or Game B?   _____

4. If only one game can be operated at a time, how long will it take four people to play both games?   _____

Bobby and Pete run a bicycle wash-'n'-wax. Bobby washes the bicycle and then Pete waxes it. Each of them takes 10 minutes.

5. How long will it take them to wash and wax 5 bicycles?   _____

6. How long will it take them to wash and wax 6 bicycles?   _____

7. How long will it take them to wash and wax 7 bicycles?   _____

8. Do you see a pattern? Using mental math, how will take the two of them to wash and wax 20 bicycles?   _____

Check the Bill

Here are some bills from restaurants where tax and tips are included. Some of these bills are incorrect. Cross out and correct each error. Hint: The tip should be figured on the cost of the dinner **before** tax.

1.

Dinner	$18.50
Tax (4%)	0.74
Tip (15%)	2.78
Total	$22.02

2.

Dinner	$15.50
Tax (3%)	0.47
Tip (15%)	1.55
Total	$17.52

3.

Dinner	$21.80
Tax ($3\frac{1}{2}$%)	0.76
Tip (15%)	3.27
Total	$27.83

4.

Dinner	$12.75
Tax ($3\frac{1}{2}$%)	0.45
Tip (15%)	1.91
Total	$15.11

5.

Dinner	$22.45
Tax (4%)	0.90
Tip (20%)	5.61
Total	$28.96

6.

Dinner	$27.95
Tax ($3\frac{1}{2}$%)	0.98
Tip (15%)	4.19
Total	$32.06

7.

Dinner	$28.52
Tax (6%)	1.17
Tip (15%)	4.28
Total	$33.97

8.

Dinner	$19.43
Tax (3%)	0.58
Tip (15%)	2.91
Total	$22.92

Name _____

Organizing Numbers

In each set you are given 4 numbers. Organize three of
the numbers to complete each sentence. The first has
been done for you. There is more than one possible
answer.

1.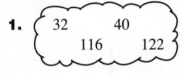

___32___ % of ___122___ is about ___40___ .

2.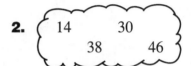

_____ % of _____ is about _____ .

3.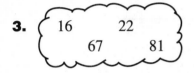

_____ % of _____ is about _____ .

4.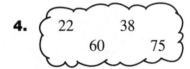

_____ % of _____ is about _____ .

5.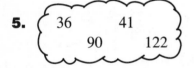

_____ % of _____ is about _____ .

6.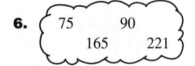

_____ % of _____ is about _____ .

7.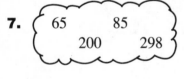

_____ % of _____ is about _____ .

8.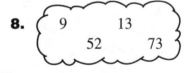

_____ % of _____ is about _____ .

9. Choose one of the exercises above. See if you can organize
the numbers differently and still have a true sentence.

_____

10. Explain why these sentences are true and the answers
are the same: 80% of 72 is about 56.
                72% of 80 is about 56.

_____

_____

Buying a Car

Carolyn wants to buy a new car. The price of the car is $8,000. The car company wants 20% down and will finance the rest at 8% interest over a period of 3 years. How much will Carolyn pay for the car?

Take 20% of $8,000 to find the down payment:
$$\$8,000 \cdot 0.2 = \$1,600$$

The down payment is $1,600.
The total cost minus the down payment gives you the amount to be financed:
$$\$8,000 - \$1,600 = \$6,400$$

To find the interest per year, take 8% of the amount financed:
$$\$6,400 \cdot 0.08 = \$512$$
The interest is $512 per year.
The interest for 3 years is $512 • 3:
$$\$512 \cdot 3 = \$1,536$$

The total cost of the car is
$8,000 + $1,536 = $9,536.
Carolyn will pay $9,536 for her new car.

Use your calculator to answer each of the following.

1. The cost of the car is $12,500. You put 35% down and finance the rest at $8\frac{1}{2}$% for 4 years. What is the total cost of the car?

_____

2. The cost of the car is $36,000. You put 25% down and finance the rest at 11% for 5 years. What is the total cost of the car?

_____

3. The cost of the car is $26,000. You put 40% down and finance the rest at 7% for 5 years. What is the total cost of the car?

_____

4. The cost of the car is $10,200. You put 50% down and finance the rest at 7.5% for 3 years. What is the total cost of the car?

_____

5. The cost of the car is $9,750. You put 15% down and finance the rest at 8% for 2 years. What is the total cost of the car?

_____

6. The cost of the car is $18,750. You put 30% down and finance the rest at 4.5% for 4 years. What is the total cost of the car?

_____

Survey

Choose one of the topics listed or make up one of your own. Make a survey of at least 30 people to gather data. Keep a list of the responses. Attach your list to this sheet.

Topics:

1. Popular First Names: The percent of students having various first names.

2. Long and Short First Names: The percent of students having first names with various numbers of letters in them.

3. Popular Pets: The percent of students with various types of pets.

4. Sibling Count: The percent of students with various numbers of children in their families.

5. My Own Topic: _____

_____

Present your findings on the survey sheet below. If you need more room, make up a sheet of your own. Share your results with the class. Round percents to the nearest half percent.

Survey of a Total _____ of People

Topic: _____

Category:	Number of People in the Category	Percent of Total Surveyed

Percent of Increase or Decrease

Pete Peterson recorded his home improvement
expenses for 7 years in this graph.

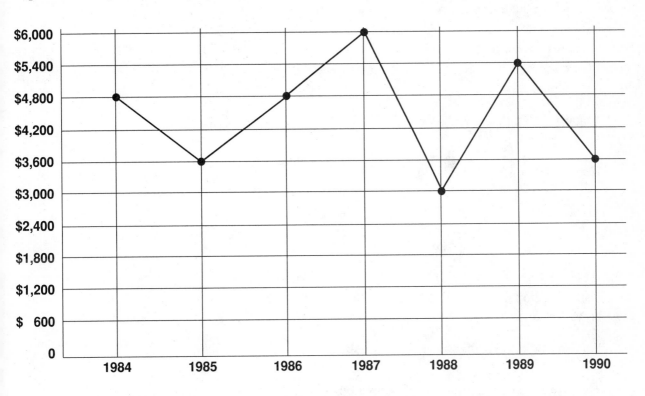

Pete wants to know the percent his expenses increased or
decreased from year to year. Complete the chart.

Year	1984	1985	1986	1987	1988	1989	1990
Expense	$4,800	$3,600					
Percent		⁻25%					

During what two-year period were Pete's expenses the
greatest? What was his percent of increase to the nearest
percent over the previous two-year period?

_____

_____

_____

_____

Competition

You manage Store B. You have read Store A's ads
and want to write your own ads for the same types of
products. Make the unit price of your products within $0.02
of your competitor's unit price. You may offer more product
for the same price or discount your prices. Then evaluate
how the sale prices of Store A and your store compare.

1. Cereal A:
   Usually 32 oz for $3.25
   Now 15% off

   Cereal B is not/is the better buy.

   The cost is _____ more/less per ounce.

   Cereal B:
   Usually 16 oz for $2.19

   Now _____

2. Pudding A:
   Usually 12 oz for 89¢
   Now 20% off

   Pudding B is not/is the better buy.

   The cost is _____ more/less per ounce.

   Pudding B:
   Usually 10 oz for 75¢

   Now _____

3. Orange Juice A:
   Usually 24 oz for $1.89
   Now 12% more for the same price

   Orange Juice B is not/is the better buy.

   The cost is _____ more/less per ounce.

   Orange Juice B:
   Usually 36 oz for $2.89

   Now _____

4. Potato Salad A:
   Usually 16 oz for $1.49
   Now 25% more for the same price

   Potato Salad B is not/is the better buy.

   The cost is _____ more/less per ounce.

   Potato Salad B:
   Usually 8 oz for 89¢

   Now _____

Name _____

Sales, Sales, Sales!

Each row of items is now at the given sale price. Find the original prices in each row. Round each to the nearest cent.

Row 1: The sale price of each item is 65% of the original price.

1. $16.85 _____

2. $69.99 _____

3. $29 _____

Row 2: The sale price of each item is 80% of the original price.

4. $1.29 _____

5. $126 _____

6. $67.88 _____

Row 3: The sale price of each item is $72\frac{1}{2}$% of the original price.

7. $5.99 _____

8. $1,450 _____

9. $37.20 _____

Row 4: The sale price of each item is $66\frac{2}{3}$% of the original price.

10. $26.89 _____

11. $439 _____

12. $620 _____

For Row 5, create your own problems similar to the ones above. Exchange them with your classmates.

Row 5: The sale price of each item is _____ of the original price.

13. _____

14. _____

15. _____

Be a Store Manager

Pretend that you are the manager of a furniture store.
The store normally prices each item at 20% above the
cost to the store. A discount for a sale comes off this
price. A chair that costs the store $100 would normally
be sold for $120. A sale discount of 15% would make
the price $102.

Solve.

1. The store buys a chair for $120. The sale
   price will be 15% off the regular price.
   What is the regular price?

   _____

   What is the sale price of the chair?

   _____

2. The store pays $375 for a television set.
   The sale price is 10% off the regular
   price. What is the sale price of the
   television?

   _____

3. You want to sell a lamp for 15% off the
   regular price. The lamp costs the store
   $95. What should the sale price be?

   _____

4. A woman buys a desk that is marked
   down from $390 to $312. What percent
   off the regular price is the sale price?

   _____

5. A man buys a table on sale for $140. That
   is 25% off the regular price. How much
   did the store pay for the table?

   _____

6. A sofa costs the store $800. You want to
   make a profit of about $65. What percent
   off the regular price should the sale price
   be?

   _____

Name _____

Making the Vote

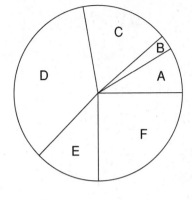

1. Look at the circle graph to the right.
Estimate the number of degrees in the
measure of each central angle of the
graph. Be sure the sum of the angles is
360°.

Angle A _____   Angle B _____

Angle C _____   Angle D _____

Angle E _____   Angle F _____

2. The circle graph shows the distribution of votes for Student Council president.
Estimate what percent of the total vote each candidate for Student Council
president received.

Candidate A _____   Candidate B _____

Candidate C _____   Candidate D _____

Candidate E _____   Candidate F _____

3. Cross-check your estimates. Multiply 360° by each percent in Exercise 2 to find the corre-
sponding number of degrees in each central angle. How close were you to your original
estimate in Exercise 1?

A_____   **B**_____

C_____   **D**_____

E_____   **F**_____

Name _____

Percent Patterns

Find 1% of each number. A calculator may be helpful.

1. 100 _____

2. 300 _____

3. 175 _____

4. 54 _____

5. 2 _____

6. 4,565 _____

7. Write a rule for finding 1% of a number.

_____

_____

Solve each of the following.

8. 1% of what number is 54?

9. 1% of what number is 0.07?

_____

_____

10. Explain the difference between Exercises 1 to 6 and Exercises 8 and 9.

_____

_____

_____

11. How did you modify your rule in Exercise 7 to help you answer Exercises 8 and 9?

_____

_____

12. Find 10% of each number in Exercises 1 to 6.

_____ , _____ , _____ , _____ , _____ , _____

13. Write a rule for finding 10% of a number.

_____

14. Are there any similarities between finding 1% of a number and finding 10% of a number?

_____

_____

What Is the Problem?

Problems may contain too much information, too little information, or contradictory information. Try to solve each problem below. If you are not given enough information, write **not enough information**. If the information is contradictory, write **no solution**.

1. Carrie works after school in the library. Her salary is $4 an hour. How much money did Carrie make last week?

   _____

2. Andy jumped 6 in. higher than Suzanne. Mary jumped 7 in. less than Andy. Bert jumped 2 in. higher than Mary. Suzanne jumped 22 in. What was the highest jump?

   _____

3. Apples cost $0.25 and pears cost $0.30. Gail purchased some of both. She gave the cashier $12. How much change did she receive?

   _____

4. Ursula purchased 4 bags of oranges. On Wednesday, she ate 2 oranges. How many oranges does she have left?

   _____

5. Bart's car gets 23 miles per gallon. Gas costs $1.05 a gallon. How many miles can Bart drive with 12 gallons?

   _____

6. Large cards come in packages of 8 and cost $2.85. Small cards come in packages of 10 and cost $2.70. Yukio purchased 7 packages of cards containing 64 cards in all. How many packages of each did he buy?

   _____

7. Baseball tickets cost $11 for the lower level, $9.50 for the middle level, and $6 for an upper deck. Mr. Torres gave the cashier $40 and received $3 change. How many of each type of ticket did he buy?

   _____

8. In his last baseball game, Danny went 3 for 5. How much did that raise his batting average?

   _____

Number Line Comparisons

For each integer, use the number line to find the 2
integers that are the given distance from the starting
point.

	Start at	Distance	Integers
1.	2	2	
2.	⁻2	2	
3.	1	4	
4.	⁻2	3	
5.	⁻1	4	
6.	⁻4	1	
7.	⁻3	1	

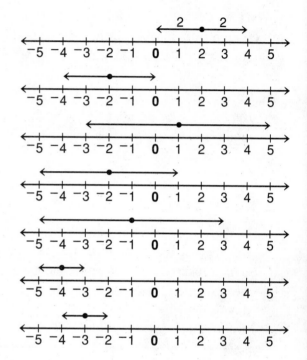

Use > or < to compare the integer pairs above.

1. ___ 0 < 4 or 4 > 0 ___

2. _____

3. _____

4. _____

5. _____

6. _____

7. _____

Exploring Equations

Use the properties of integers to solve each equation.

1. $^+14 + (^-14 + ^+3) = w$

w = _____

2. $^+22\,(^+6 + ^-6) = k$

k = _____

3. $^+5 \cdot (x + ^-7) = ^+5$

x = _____

4. $^-13 + (m - ^+2) = 0$

m = _____

5. $z + (^+3 + ^-3) = ^+9$

z = _____

6. $(p + ^-2) \cdot ^+13 = ^+13$

p = _____

7. $^+8 + (y + ^-8) = ^+16$

y = _____

8. $^+19\,(d + ^-4) = 0$

d = _____

9. $(t + ^+11) \cdot ^+5 = 0$

t = _____

10. $^+12\,(v + ^+16) = 0$

v = _____

11. $^+19 + (b + ^+6) = ^+6$

b = _____

12. $^+7 + (^+10 + a) = ^+10$

a = _____

13. $(^+1 + ^+25 + f) \cdot ^+20 = ^+20$

f = _____

14. $^+13\,(^-36 + ^+1 + k) = ^+13$

k = _____

15. $^+16 + (g + ^+8) = ^+160$

g = _____

16. $^+10\,(m + ^-3) + ^-3 = ^+17$

m = _____

Integer Squares

Complete the square at the right using counting chips and the following steps:

► Add across.
► Add down.
► Add your sums across and down.
► Write your sums in the triangles.

What did you find about the numbers in the

triangles? _____

1.

$^+4$	$^-3$	$=$ ____
$^-5$	$^+6$	$=$ ____
$=$	$=$	

_____ _____

Complete the squares below. Use counting chips if necessary.

2.

$^-8$	$^+4$	$=$ ____
$^+10$	$^-5$	$=$ ____
$=$	$=$	

_____ _____

3.

$^+7$	$^-7$	$=$ ____
$^-5$	$^+5$	$=$ ____
$=$	$=$	

_____ _____

4.

$^+2$	$^-8$	$=$ ____
$^+3$	$^+6$	$=$ ____
$=$	$=$	

_____ _____

5.

$^-1$	$^-2$	$=$ ____
$^-3$	$^-4$	$=$ ____
$=$	$=$	

_____ _____

Name _____

Very Variable

Evaluate each algebraic expression for the values given.

1. $x - 8$

$x = 12$ _____ $x = 6$ _____

2. $t - 32$

$t = {}^- 6$ _____ $t = 17$ _____

3. $y - {}^- 11$

$y = {}^- 11$ _____ $y = {}^- 5$ _____

4. $m - {}^- 4$

$m = 3$ _____ $m = {}^- 10$ _____

5. $16 - j$

$j = 22$ _____ $j = {}^- 9$ _____

6. ${}^- 18 - k$

$k = {}^- 20$ _____ $k = 7$ _____

7. $q + {}^- 43$

$q = 42$ _____ $q = {}^- 15$ _____

8. ${}^- z + 23$

$z = 14$ _____ $z = {}^- 2$ _____

9. $37 - {}^- w$

$w = 1$ _____ $w = 18$ _____

10. $92 - n$

$n = 108$ _____ $n = {}^- 19$ _____

11. $45 + ({}^- a - c)$

$a = 12$ and $c = 23$ _____

$a = {}^- 2$ and $c = {}^- 14$ _____

12. $22 - (v - h)$

$v = 6$ and $h = {}^- 17$ _____

$v = {}^- 21$ and $h = {}^- 11$ _____

13. $p - ({}^- 3 + r)$

$p = 38$ and $r = 41$ _____

$p = {}^- 29$ and $r = 7$ _____

14. $(f + 16) - g$

$f = {}^- 34$ and $g = {}^- 41$ _____

$f = {}^- 15$ and $g = {}^- 5$ _____

Perplexing Patterns

Look at each sequence of integers and find the
patterns. Predict the next integers for each sequence.

Sequence	**Pattern**

1. 3, 6, 12, 24, _____ , _____ , _____   Multiply by 2.

2. 3, ⁻6, 12, ⁻24, _____ , _____ , _____   _____

3. 2, 8, 32, _____ , _____ , _____   _____

4. 2, ⁻8, 32, _____ , _____ , _____   _____

5. 4, ⁻4, 4, ⁻4, _____ , _____ , _____   _____

6. 2, 2, 4, 4, 12, 12, _____ , _____   _____

7. 2, ⁻2, ⁻4, 4, 12, ⁻12, _____ , _____   _____

8. 64, 32, 16, 8, _____ , _____ , _____   _____

9. ⁻64, 32, ⁻16, 8, _____ , _____ , _____   _____

Solve. Use the patterns for the multiplication of
positive and negative integers.

10. ⁻2 • 3 • ⁻1 • ⁻2 • 3 • ⁻1 • ⁻1 • 2 • ⁻3 • 2 • ⁻1 • ⁻1 _____

11. ⁻1 • 1 • ⁻1 • 2 • ⁻2 • 2 • ⁻3 • 3 • ⁻3   _____

12. ⁻4 • 5 • 0 • ⁻1 • ⁻8 • 2   _____

Multiplication Madness

Look at other patterns of integer multiplication

1. $6 \cdot {}^-18 =$ _____

2. $({}^-2 \cdot 5) \cdot 3 =$ _____

3. $(4 \cdot {}^-6) \cdot 7 =$ _____

4. $(8 \cdot 9)(2 \cdot {}^-1) =$ _____

5. Each problem above has _____ negative factor.

6. Each product is _____ .

7. ${}^-17 \cdot {}^-3 =$ _____

8. $({}^-6 \cdot 5) \cdot {}^-8 =$ _____

9. $(9 \cdot {}^-2)({}^-3 \cdot 1) =$ _____

10. $({}^-4 \cdot {}^-7)(2 \cdot 2) =$ _____

11. Each problem above has _____ negative factors.

12. Each product is _____ .

13. $({}^-5 \cdot {}^-4) \cdot {}^-7 =$ _____

14. ${}^-3 \cdot ({}^-8 \cdot {}^-2) =$ _____

15. $({}^-3 \cdot {}^-4)({}^-2 \cdot 8) =$ _____

16. $({}^-10 \cdot 1)({}^-7 \cdot {}^-1) =$ _____

17. Each problem above has _____ negative factors.

18. Each product is _____ .

19. $({}^-3 \cdot {}^-5)({}^-2 \cdot {}^-2) =$ _____

20. $({}^-9 \cdot {}^-1)({}^-4 \cdot {}^-3) =$ _____

21. $({}^-6 \cdot {}^-1)({}^-4 \cdot {}^-11) =$ _____

22. $({}^-20 \cdot {}^-5)({}^-3 \cdot {}^-6) =$ _____

23. Each problem above has _____ negative factors.

24. Each product is _____ .

25. Draw a conclusion about the product of positive and negative integers.

_____

_____

Use your conclusion to solve this problem.

26. ${}^-1 \times {}^-2 \times {}^-3 \times {}^-4 \times {}^-5 \times {}^-6 =$ _____

Division Decisions

Look for a pattern in the division of positive and
negative integers. Before you find the answers, answer
questions 1, 7, 13, and 17.

1. Each of exercises 2 through 5 has

_____ negative sign.

2. $24 \div {}^-6$ _____

3. $^-35 \div 5$ _____

4. $(81 \div {}^-9) \div 3$ _____

5. $(125 \div 5) \div {}^-5$ _____

6. Each quotient is _____ .

7. Each of exercises 8 through 11 has

_____ negative signs.

8. $^-51 \div {}^-3$ _____

9. $^-64 \div {}^-8$ _____

10. $(16 \div {}^-2) \div {}^-4$ _____

11. $^-96 \div ({}^-42 \div 7)$ _____

12. Each quotient is _____ .

13. Each of exercises 14 and 15 has

_____ negative signs.

14. $(^-80 \div {}^-4) \div {}^-5$ _____

15. $(^-45 \div {}^-3) \div (^-20 \div 4)$ _____

16. Each quotient is _____ .

17. Each of exercises 18 and 19 has

_____ negative signs.

18. $(^-100 \div {}^-2) \div (^-16 \div {}^-8)$ _____

19. $(^-49 \div {}^-7) \div (^-56 \div {}^-8)$ _____

20. Each quotient is _____ .

21. Draw a conclusion about the quotient of positive and
negative integers.

_____

_____

Work from left to right. Use your conclusion above to
solve this problem.

22. $^-600 \div {}^-2 \div {}^-3 \div {}^-2 \div {}^-2 \div {}^-5 \div {}^-5$ _____

Thinking Graphs

On the rectangular coordinate system below, draw the
graph for each *x*-coordinate and *y*-coordinate
relationship indicated.

1. The *y*-coordinate is 0, and the product of the coordinates is 0.

2. The *x*-coordinate is 5 more than the *y*-coordinate.

3. The sum of the coordinates is 5.

4. Look at the three lines. What ordered pair appears on all the lines? _____

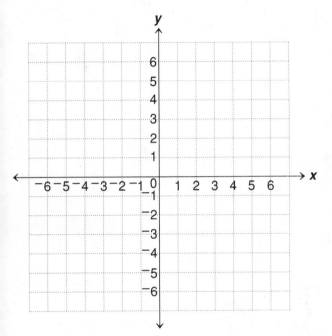

5. Make up a relationship between *x*-and *y*-coordinates. Graph all the points that meet the relationship.

_____

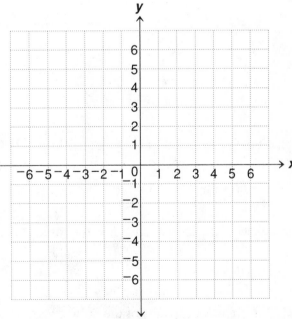

Equating Equations

Graph the three equations on the axes below.
Label each line graph.

$$y = 2x - 4 \qquad y = -\frac{1}{2} + 1 \qquad y = x - 5$$

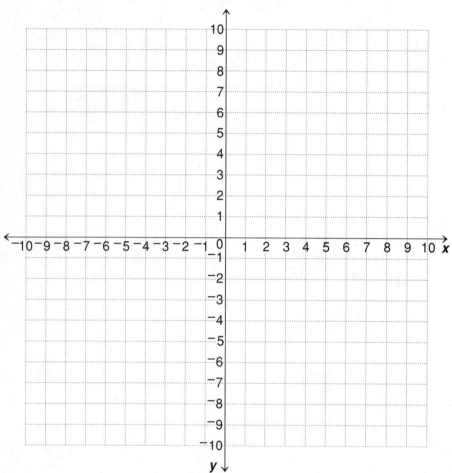

1. What is the point of intersection for $y = 2x - 4$ and $y = x - 5$? _____

2. What is the point of intersection for $y = 2x - 4$ and $y = -\frac{1}{2}x + 1$? _____

3. What is the point of intersection for $y = x - 5$ and $y = -\frac{1}{2}x + 1$? _____

Shade the area that is bounded by the three equations.

4. What type of polygon is the area? _____

5. Give the coordinates of the polygon's vertices. _____

Name _____

Who Is On?

Below are the work schedules of 4 employees of a
frozen yogurt store. All of them are working on
October 1, and all four are trying to figure out who
works with whom and when for the rest of the month.
Help them solve their dilemma. Be sure to check for
more than one solution.

EMPLOYEE	DAYS	TIME
Joey	every other day	1:00 - 8:00 p.m.
Debbie	every third day	12:00 - 7:00 p.m.
Eddie	every fourth day	2:00 - 9:00 p.m.
Melanie	every sixth day	3:00 - 10:00 p.m.

1. On what day, other than October 1, will
all four of them be working together?

_____

2. Who will be working together on
October 5?

_____

3. On what days will only Eddie and Joey be
working together?

_____

4. On what days will only Joey, Debbie, and
Melanie be working together?

_____

5. Why is it that every day that Melanie
works, so do Joey and Debbie?

_____

_____

_____

6. On October 13 at 7:30 p.m., who will be
working?

_____

7. On October 13 at 2:25 p.m., who will be
working?

_____

Chance Events and Numerical Values

The line below can be used to rate the likelihood of an event occurring. It assigns numerical values to chance events. 0 corresponds to Impossible and 1 corresponds to Certain.

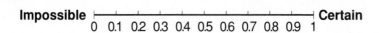

Impossible ├──┬──┬──┬──┬──┬──┬──┬──┬──┬──┤ Certain
0 0.1 0.2 0.3 0.4 0.5 0.6 0.7 0.8 0.9 1

The line above and the spinner below are both divided into 10 equal segments. Using the line, assign a numerical value to each event. Assume that the spinner will not land on a line. Exercise 1 has been completed for you.

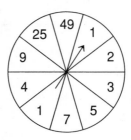

1. Spinning a 3 __0.1__

2. Spinning an odd number _____

3. Spinning a 10 _____

4. Spinning a 1 _____

5. Spinning a number less than 7 _____

6. Spinning a number greater than or equal to 9 _____

7. Spinning a 1, 2, 3, 5, 7, 4, 9, 25, or 49 _____

8. Spinning 25 or 49 _____

9. Spinning an even number _____

10. Spinning a square number _____

Mealtime Probabilities

Dear Family,
    We have been studying probability. This unit deals with sample spaces, the list of all possible outcomes for an experiment. You can prepare a list of 4 main dishes, 3 vegetables, and 3 desserts that your family likes. Make a one-letter abbreviation for each type of food. Make a list of all the 3-part meals that could be prepared from these choices. Complete the sample first.

Sample:

Fried Chicken **F**	Broccoli **B**	Ice Cream **I**
Hamburger **H**	Carrots **C**	Apple Pie **A**
Steak **S**	Peas **P**	Yogurt **Y**
Macaroni and Cheese **M**		

(F,B,I), (F,C,I), (F,P,I), _____

_____

_____

_____

_____

1. How many outcomes did you list?

_____

2. Circle your 3 favorite meals from among the choices above. What is the mathematical probability that you will have one of the meals you circled?

_____

3. The mathematical probability of an event and the actual probability are often different due to outside factors. Are there any meals listed above that are not as likely to be prepared as the remaining ones? _____ Explain.

_____

_____

This information could change the probability you found in Exercise 2. Does it affect the probability of having one of

your 3 favorite meals? _____
If your answer is yes, does the probability

increase or decrease? _____

Why? _____

_____

_____

_____

Fruit Basket Turnover

Discover how the probability of an event is affected if objects are drawn randomly and not replaced. Answer the questions below.

A covered basket contains 2 peaches, 3 apples, 3 plums, and 4 pears.

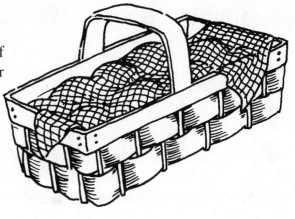

1. Kara is allergic to peaches. What is the probability of her reaching into the covered basket and randomly selecting a piece of fruit she can eat?

_____

2. What is the probability of reaching into the covered basket and randomly selecting:

a peach? _____

a pear? _____

an apple? _____

a plum? _____

3. Kara's friend, Julia, ate 2 plums and a pear from the covered basket. What is the new probability of randomly selecting:

a peach? _____

a pear? _____

an apple? _____

a plum? _____

a piece of fruit that Kara can eat?

_____

4. Compare your answers in Problems 2 and 3. Which probability remained the same although

Julia ate some of the fruit? _____

Why? _____

_____

5. Which probabilities increased after Julia ate the fruit? _____

Why? _____

6. Which probabilities decreased after Julia ate the fruit? _____

Why? _____

_____

_____

Name _____

It's a Toss-Up

Toss a coin 12 times. Make a check (✓) beside
"Tails" each time a tail appears and beside "Heads"
each time a head appears. To generate the next row,
write the total number of tails (or heads) you have
obtained so far over the number of tosses. Find the
percent by dividing the numerator by the denominator
and rounding to the nearest whole number.

Tosses	1	2	3	4	5	6	7	8	9	10	11	12
Tails												
Total tails/tosses												
Percent												
Heads												
Total heads/tosses												
Percent												

Make a double line graph to show your results. Use
a solid line for the percent of tails obtained. Use a
dotted line for the percent of heads.

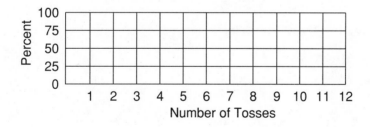

Analyze the graph. What do you notice?

_____

_____

_____

_____

Name _____

Is There a Quicker Way?

There are 4 shirts (1 aqua, 1 plum, 1 navy, and 1 tan) to be displayed side by side in a store window. List the different ways they can be arranged.

_____

_____

_____

_____

1. How many different arrangements are there? _____

2. Look at the expressions below. Which represents the

number of arrangements in Exercise 1? _____

    A $4 \times 2 \times 1$ **B** $5 \times 3 \times 2 \times 1$

    C $4 \times 3 \times 2 \times 1$ **D** $4 \times 3 \times 1$

There are 3 hats (black, navy, and pin-striped). List the different ways they could be set side by side on a closet shelf. _____

_____

3. How many different arrangements are there? _____

4. Look at the expressions below. Which one represents

the number of arrangements in Exercise 3? _____

    A $3 \times 3 \times 2 \times 1$ **B** $3 \times 2 \times 1$

    C 3×3 **D** $3 \times 3 \times 2 \times 2 \times 1$

An expression such as $6 \times 5 \times 4 \times 3 \times 2 \times 1$ is written 6! and is read "six factorial." To determine the number of arrangements of n objects when the order of the objects is important, find n!

5. Write out 7! to predict how many different arrangements could be made if 7 brands of pens are

to be displayed side by side on a shelf. _____

6. Use a calculator to compute 7! _____

Too Big and Too Little

You are supposed to take your 8-year-old cousin Karen to the amusement park.
She has been complaining that the kiddie rides are too babyish and that she
cannot go on most of the big rides. Karen is 4 ft 5 in. tall.

Make graphs on the number lines of the age and height restrictions for the big rides.
Label each graph with the name of the ride.

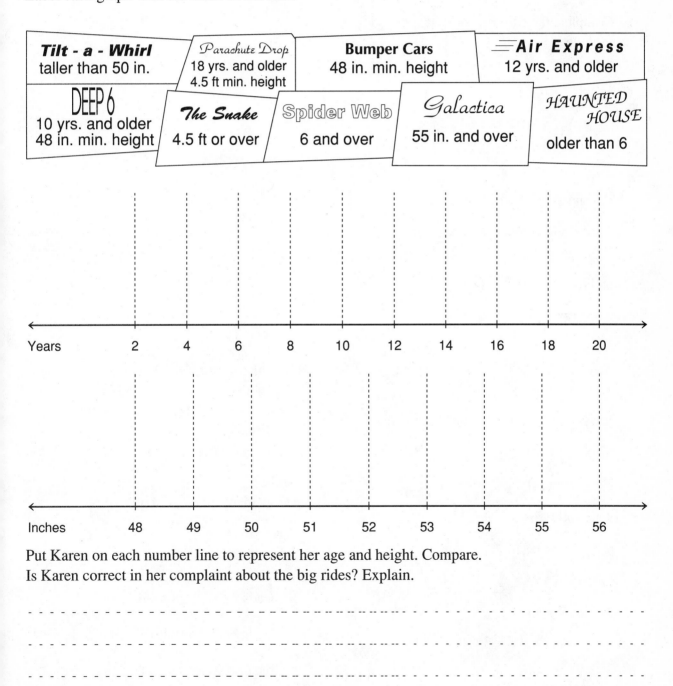

Tilt - a - Whirl
taller than 50 in.

Parachute Drop
18 yrs. and older
4.5 ft min. height

Bumper Cars
48 in. min. height

Air Express
12 yrs. and older

DEEP 6
10 yrs. and older
48 in. min. height

The Snake
4.5 ft or over

Spider Web
6 and over

Galactica
55 in. and over

HAUNTED HOUSE
older than 6

Years   2   4   6   8   10   12   14   16   18   20

Inches   48   49   50   51   52   53   54   55   56

Put Karen on each number line to represent her age and height. Compare.
Is Karen correct in her complaint about the big rides? Explain.

Name _____

Pascal's Triangle

The "triangle" of numbers at the right, called Pascal's triangle, is an indicator of probabilities for certain experiments. Notice that each "outside" number is a 1 and that every other number is the result of adding the two numbers above it.

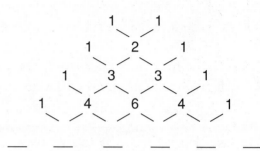

1. Complete the fifth row of Pascal's triangle.

Compare and Analyze

2. At the right is a tree diagram that shows the outcomes if a fair coin is tossed 3 times.

   How many outcomes are there ? _____
   How many chances are there of getting

   no heads? _____ 1 head? _____

   2 heads? _____ 3 heads? _____

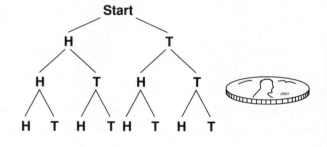

3. Now look at the third row of Pascal's triangle.

   What is the sum of the numbers on the

   third row? _____

   From left to right,

   what is the first number? _____

   second number? _____

   third number? _____

   fourth number? _____

4. A fair coin is tossed 4 times. Rather than drawing a tree diagram, look at the fourth row of Pascal's triangle. Answer the questions.
   How many possible outcomes

   exist? _____
   How many chances of getting

   no heads? _____

   1 head? _____ 2 heads? _____

   3 heads? _____ 4 heads? _____

   What is the probability of getting 3 heads

   in the above experiment? _____

132   Use with text pages 354–355.   **TS-7**

Solve Related Problems

Related problems can be solved using the same
strategies. Solve each problem. State what strategy you
used. Write a related problem in the spaces to the right.

1. Marla spent $41 for a shirt and a pair of
jeans. The jeans cost $4 more than the
shirt. How much did the jeans cost?

_____

Strategy: _____

2. Mr. Joyce divides his marble collection
among his 4 children. The oldest gets $\frac{1}{2}$
the marbles. The second child gets $\frac{1}{4}$ of
the marbles. The third child gets $\frac{1}{8}$ of the
marbles, and the youngest gets 500. How
many marbles did Mr. Joyce originally
have?

_____

Strategy: _____

3. Brenda has 6 solid blouses, 6 striped
blouses, 4 print blouses, and 3 other
blouses. She keeps only blouses in her
drawer. If she reaches into the drawer
without looking and selects a blouse, what
is the probability she will get a striped
blouse?

_____

Strategy: _____

Name _____

Spin Off

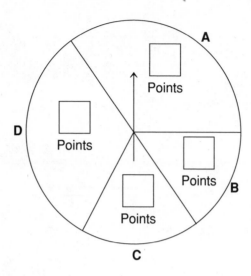

$$P(A) = \frac{1}{3} \qquad P(B) = \frac{1}{6} \qquad P(C) = \frac{1}{6} \qquad P(D) = \frac{1}{3}$$

The arrow is spun 60 times. The probability of landing on each part of the spinner is listed above, but the points assigned to each are missing. Using the information below, complete the table and write the correct numbers on the spinner.

	Outcome	Number Expected in 60 Spins	Total Points
A			40
B			30
C			40
D			100
	Total of All Spins		
	Expected Value		

Name _____

Pick's Formula: Area of Polygons

Here is a formula for determining the area of polygons on a geoboard. It is called Pick's formula. $A = \left(\dfrac{B}{2} + I \right) - 1$

A = area
B = number of border nails
I = number of interior nails

Example:

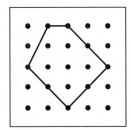

$B = 8, I = 6$
$A = \left(\dfrac{8}{2} + 6 \right) - 1$
$A = \left(4 + 6 \right) - 1 = 9$
The area is 9 square units.

Find the area of each polygon below.

1.

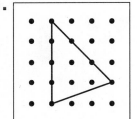

$A =$ _____

2.

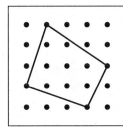

$A =$ _____

3.

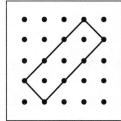

$A =$ _____

4.

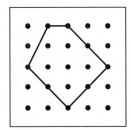

$A =$ _____

5.

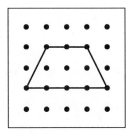

$A =$ _____

6.

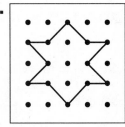

$A =$ _____

7.

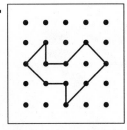

$A =$ _____

8.

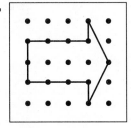

$A =$ _____

9.

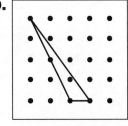

$A =$ _____

Area Comparison

Look at the given figures. What is the result of the
changes in dimensions?

A parallelogram has a base of 20 m and a height of 8 m

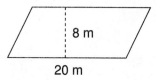

1. What is the area? _____

2. Two meters may be added to either the base or to the height of this

parallelogram. Which would result in a greater area? _____

3. Which would give a greater change in the area of the

parallelogram—adding 7 m to the base or adding 3 m to the height? _____

A rectangle has a length of 7 cm and a width of 4.5 cm

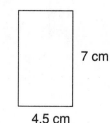

4. What is the area? _____ What is the perimeter? _____

5. Add 3.5 cm to the width. What is the change in the

perimeter of the rectangle? _____ What is the change in the area? _____

6. Add 3.5 cm to the length. What is the change in the perimeter of the

rectangle? _____ What is the change in the area? _____

7. Subtract 0.5 cm from the width. What is the change in the perimeter of the

rectangle? _____ What is the change in the area? _____

8. Subtract 0.5 cm from the length. What is the change in the perimeter of the

rectangle? _____ What is the change in the area? _____

9. Add 0.5 cm to the length. What is the change in the area? _____

Name _____

Special Triangles and Trapezoids

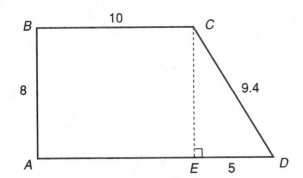

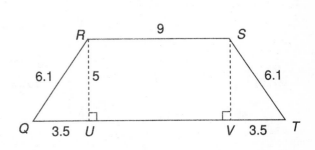

Look at trapezoid *ABCE*. This is special because one of its nonparallel sides, *BA*, is perpendicular to the bases.

1. The area of rectangle *ABCE* is

_____

The area of triangle *CDE* is

_____

2. Add these two areas together to get the area of trapezoid *ABC*.

_____

3. Use the formula to find the area of trapezoid *ABC*.

_____

4. What information given in the diagram is not necessary in order to determine any of these areas?

_____

Look at trapezoid *QRST*. This is another special trapezoid. A triangle with two equal sides has the same name as this trapezoid.

5. What is it?

_____

6. What is the area of rectangle *RSVU*?

_____

7. What is the area of triangle *RUQ*?

_____

Triangle *STV*?

_____

8. Add these three areas to get the area of trapezoid *QRST*.

_____

9. Use the formula to compute the area of trapezoid *QRST*.

_____

Bullseye

Concentric circles are circles that share the same
center. The diameters of the four concentric circles are
given below. Determine the radius and area for each
one. Round to the nearest hundredth.

Circle	Diameter	Radius	Area
A	0.5 cm	_____	_____
B	1.5 cm	_____	_____
C	3.25 cm	_____	_____
D	5 cm	_____	_____

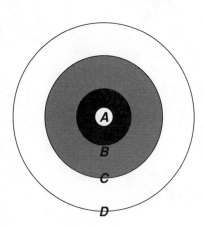

1. Look at Circle *B*. Circle *A* lies in the interior of
   Circle *B*. How can you find the area of the shaded
   region of Circle *B*?

   _____

2. What is the area of the shaded region of Circle *B*? _____

3. What is the area of the dotted region of Circle *C*? _____

4. What is the area of the outer blank region of Circle *D*? _____

Cutouts

Look at the figure below. All circles are the same size, with $r = 6$ cm.

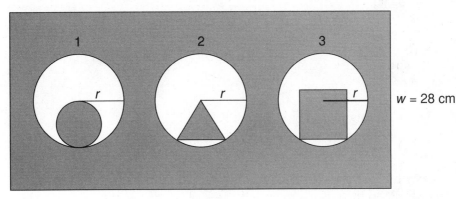

$l = 46$ cm

1. If the inner circle with $r = 3$ cm is removed,
find the area of Circle 1.   _____

2. If the triangle with $b = 4$ cm, $h = 4.5$ cm is
removed, find the area of Circle 2.   _____

3. If the square with $s = 6.5$ cm is removed,
find the area of Circle 3.   _____

4. What is the area of the rectangle with the
three circles removed?   _____

5. What is the area of the shaded part of the
figure?   _____

Look at the square at the right.

6. Find the area of the unshaded figure.

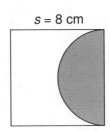

$s = 8$ cm

_____

Mixed Bag

Solve. Use any problem solving strategy.

1. Gene purchased a carpet that was on sale for $15 per square yard. He paid $450. What were the dimensions of the carpet if twice the width minus 0.5 yards was the length?

_____

2. Donean was planning a party. Each time that Donean invited one person, that person invited two people, and each of those two people invited two more people. If Donean herself invited 8 people to the party, how many guests will she have in all at her party?

_____

3. The length of a rectangular kitchen is 5 feet greater than the width. The perimeter of the room is 46 feet. If the total cost to put tiling on the floor is $630, what is the cost of the tiles per square foot?

_____

4. The sum of three consecutive even numbers is 162. What are the three numbers?

_____

5. Jana and Hector were playing tennis on a regular court that was 78 feet long. Starting from the baseline, Hector hit a ball 45 feet. Jana returned the ball by hitting it 15 feet. From that point on, each of them hit the ball 8 feet farther than the last person. Who was the first person to hit the ball out of bounds?

_____

6. Assume you have a balance scale and three weights—1 oz, 3 oz, and 9 oz—that you can place on either side of the scale. You also have objects ranging in weight from 1 oz to 13 oz in 1-oz increments. Which objects can you weigh with the weights that you have?

_____

Name _____

Maximum Space

Solve. Then look for a pattern in your answers.

1. A rectangle with a perimeter of 24 cm has the greatest

possible area. Its dimensions are: _____

2. A rectangle with a perimeter of 40 m has the greatest

possible area. Its dimensions are: _____

3. A rectangle with a perimeter of 60 m has the greatest

possible area. Its dimensions are: _____

4. What can you conclude about rectangles and

maximum area? _____

_____

Use mental math and your conclusion above to solve
the following problems.

5. A rectangle with a perimeter of 320,000 ft has the

greatest possible area. Its dimensions are: _____

6. What is the maximum area of a rectangle with a

perimeter of 8 in.? _____

7. A rectangle with a perimeter of 0.16 m has the

greatest possible area. Its dimensions are: _____

What is the maximum area of this rectangle? _____

Does this mean that the area of this rectangle is $\frac{1}{100}$

of the perimeter? Explain. _____

_____

Name _____

Trapezoid Tangle

Find the height of the trapezoid at the right. _____

You know how to use the formula for the area of a
trapezoid when the unknown is the area or the height.
How do you find the unknown when it is one of the
bases?

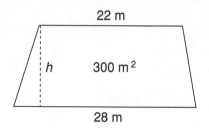

22 m

h 300 m^2

28 m

Using the techniques of solving equations, complete
the steps to rewrite the formula for the area of a
trapezoid to solve for b_1.

$$A = \rule{3cm}{0.4pt}$$

$$2A = \rule{3cm}{0.4pt}$$

$$\rule{3cm}{0.4pt} = b_1 + b_2$$

$$\rule{3cm}{0.4pt} = b_1$$

Now rewrite the formula to solve for b_2.

_____

Solve for the missing bases.

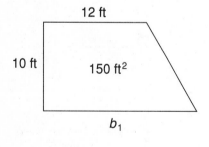

12 ft

10 ft   150 ft^2

b_1

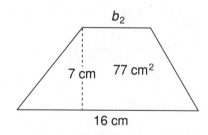

b_2

7 cm   77 cm^2

16 cm

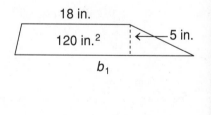

18 in.

120 in.^{2} 5 in.

b_1

1. _____   **2.** _____   **3.** _____

Surface Area

Find the approximate cost of fabric needed to cover
the outside of each shape if fabric costs $5.50 per
square meter.

1. A rectangular prism with $h = 6$ m, $w = 7$ m, and $l = 12$ m _____

2. A cylinder with $r = 2$ m and $h = 30$ m _____

3. An open cylinder with $r = 6$ m and $h = 3$ m _____

Solve.

4. Two trunks shaped like rectangular prisms are to be
lined with wallpaper that costs $8.50 per square foot.
How much more will it cost to line the larger one with
$h = 3$ ft, $l = 6$ ft, and $w = 2$ ft than the smaller one with
$h = 3$ ft, $l = 4$ ft, and $w = 2$ ft? _____

5. Cylindrical cereal boxes with $r = 2$ in. and $h = 7$ in.
are to be painted. If a 12-oz jar of paint covers 400 in.^{2},
how many jars should you buy to paint 50 cereal boxes? _____

6. A doghouse shaped like a rectangular prism has $l = 5$ ft,
$w = 2.5$ ft, $h = 3$ ft, and an opening of 2 ft by 1.5 ft. Will
paint that covers 125 ft^2 be enough for the walls, ceiling
and floor of the doghouse? Justify your answer. _____

Cubic Addition

Look at the figure at the right.

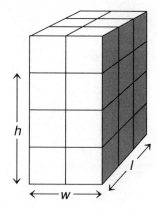

1. What is the height? _____ The width? _____

   The length? _____

2. What is the volume of the figure? _____

3. Subtract 3 units from the height, 1 unit from the width, and 2 units from the length. What is the volume?

   _____

4. What would the volume be if 1 unit were added to the height? _____

5. What would the volume be if 1 unit were added to the width? _____

6. What would the volume be if 1 unit were added to the length? _____

7. What would the volume be if 1 unit were added to the length, the width, and the height? _____

8. Can you draw any conclusions about the relationship between the dimensions of the figure and the

   volume? _____

9. Adding 1 unit to which dimension caused the greatest

   change in volume? _____

   Explain. _____

Base-ic Volume

The volume of any prism is equal to the area of the base, B, times the height of the prism (h). $V = Bh$

Use these area formulas to help you find the volume of the prisms given below.

Area of a **triangle**: $A = \frac{1}{2} bh$

Area of a **rectangle**: $A = lw$

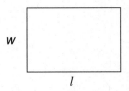

Area of a **parallelogram**: $A = b \times h$

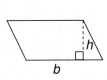

Area of a **regular hexagon**:
A is approximately $0.072\, p^2$
(p is the perimeter of the hexagon)

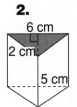

Find the volume. The shading shows the base of each figure.

1.

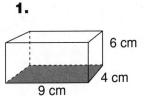

Area of base = _____

Volume of prism = _____

2.

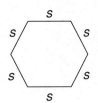

Area of base = _____

Volume of prism = _____

3.

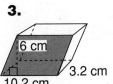

Area of base = _____

Volume of prism = _____

4.

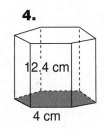

Area of base = _____

Volume of prism = _____

Name _____

Thinking Capacity

You can measure liquids in milliliters

       1 milliliter = 1 cubic centimeter

Estimate how many milliliters each can contains. Then calculate the actual capacity using the formula for the area of a cylinder. Compare.

A
5 cm
r = 3 cm

B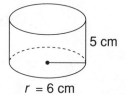
5 cm
r = 6 cm

C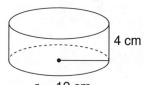
4 cm
r = 12 cm

D
8 cm
r = 12 cm

	Volume (cm³) or Capacity (mL)		
Container		Estimated	Actual
A			
B			
C			
D			

Solve the problems. Then complete the chart.

1. Estimate the capacity of B if the height is doubled.

_____

2. Estimate the capacity of container B if the radius is doubled.

_____

3. Estimate the capacity of container C if the height is cut in half.

_____

4. Estimate the capacity of container C if the radius is cut in half.

_____

5. What is the capacity of container A if the height is multiplied by 10? Use mental math.

_____

6. What is the capacity of container A if the radius is multiplied by 10? Use mental math.

Explain. _____

_____

_____

Name _____

Cubic Comparisons

A pyramid and a cone are each inscribed in cubes whose edges are 8 dm long.

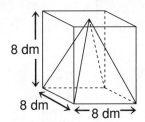 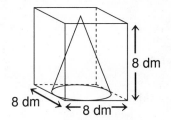

1. Find the differences for the following volumes:

V cube _____ – V pyramid _____ = _____

V cube _____ – V cone _____ = _____

V pyramid _____ – V cone _____ = _____

Add 4 dm to the length, height, and width of the cubes.

2. Compare the increases in volume:

V cube _____ – V pyramid _____ = _____

V cube _____ – V cone _____ = _____

V pyramid _____ – V cone _____ = _____

3. How much does the volume of the cube increase? _____

4. How much does the volume of the cone increase? _____

5. How much does the volume of the pyramid increase? _____

Double the length, width, and height of the cubes.

6. What happens to the volume of the cube? Use mental math. _____

7. What happens to the volume of the pyramid? _____

8. What happens to the volume of the cone? _____

Name _____

Brush up on Your Mathematics

Use the blueprint of Juanita's current remodeling job to answer the questions below.

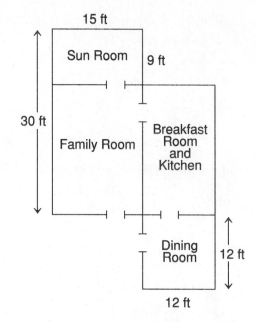

1. The family room floor is to have a pecan polyurethane finish. The manufacturer advises that 1 pint of finish will cover 60 square feet. How many pint cans should Juanita buy? _____

2. Juanita is going to paint the sun room with a pearl white latex paint. One gallon of this paint will over 400 square feet. the sun room ceiling is 8 feet high. Use Juanita's worksheet below to figure out how many cans of paint she should buy to cover the 4 walls and the ceiling.

Ceiling area: _____ × _____ = _____ × 1 = _____

Long wall area: _____ × _____ = _____ × 2 = _____

Short wall area: _____ × _____ = _____ × 2 = _____

Total area _____

Deduct door and window area. **– 76 sq ft**

_____

Number of cans of paint needed: _____

3. Juanita's customers have chosen a wall-to-wall carpet for the dining room. How many square yards of carpet will she need to purchase? _____

4. The breakfast room and kitchen will have a black-and-white linoleum floor. Each 1-foot square of the pattern is a separate tile. How many tiles will Juanita need? _____

Name _____

Designs and Line Symmetry

1. The design at the right is line–symmetric. One half is a reflection of the other half. The two halves are exactly alike and fit on each other when the design is folded correctly.

Draw lines of symmetry through the design to show where it could be folded.

2. Draw lines of symmetry through this design:

3. Make two line–symmetric designs of your own on these grids. Remember to keep your line or lines of symmetry in mind.

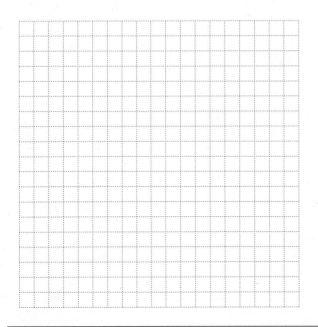

Name _____

Reflections in the Coordinate Plane

Draw the reflection image of each figure. Then write
the coordinates of the vertices of each new figure.

1.

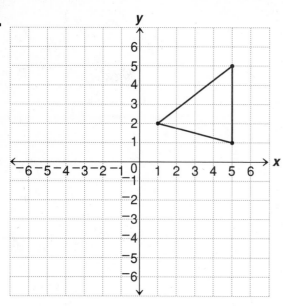

2.

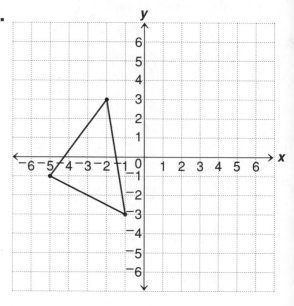

3.

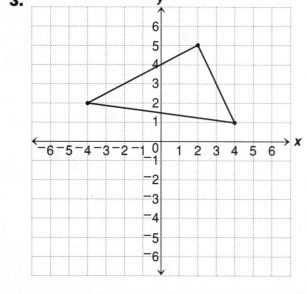

4.

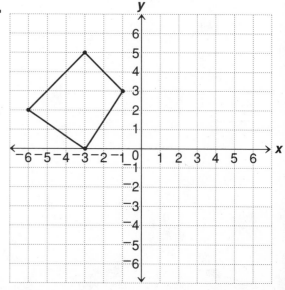

Turn Symmetry and Regular Polygons

A regular polygon is a polygon in which all sides have
the same length and all angles have the same measure.

Describe the turn symmetry of each regular polygon.

1. regular triangle: _____   **2.** square: _____

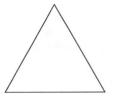

3. regular pentagon: _____   **4.** regular hexagon: _____

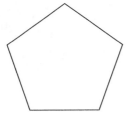 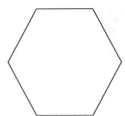

5. What do you notice about the turn symmetry of each
regular polygon as the number of sides increase?

_____

_____

_____

6. Use your answer from Problem 5 to
predict the turn symmetry for a regular
octagon. Then draw a regular octagon and
verify your prediction.

_____

Alphabet Rotations

Tell whether each letter's $\frac{1}{2}$- turn image about Point 0
is a letter of the alphabet. Then tell if the letter's
$\frac{1}{2}$- turn image is the same or a different letter. If it
is a different letter, write that letter.

1.
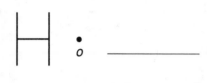
_____

_____

2.

_____

_____

3.
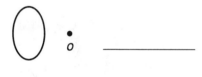
_____

_____

4.

_____

_____

5.

_____

_____

6.

_____

_____

7. For which letters is a $\frac{1}{4}$- turn image a
letter of the alphabet?

_____

8. For which letter is a $\frac{1}{3}$- turn image still the
same letter?

_____

Writing Algebraic Equations

Write the algebraic equation that satisfies the values of
x and y for each table.

1.

x	0	2	10	20	300
y	0	2	10	20	300

_____

2.

x	0	1	2	10	25
y	0	1	4	100	625

_____

3.

x	0	1	2	10	100
y	0	4	16	400	40,000

_____

4.

x	0	1	5	10	100
y	-1	0	24	99	9,999

_____

5.

x	0	1	2	3	4
y	100	101	104	109	116

_____

6.

x	0	1	2	3	4
y	-2	0	6	16	30

_____

7.

x	0	1	5	10	12
y	5	0	120	495	715

_____

8.

x	0	1	2	3	4
y	0	2	6	12	20

_____

9. Choose one of the exercises and explain how you arrived
at the algebraic equation.

_____

Diagram the Volume

The volume or capacity of a container is the number of
unit cubes that fit inside the container.
In each exercise below you are given the
measurements for a container. Follow steps A–E.

   A Sketch the container, then sketch unit cubes to represent the volume.
   B Find the volume.
   C Draw a sketch of the new container.
   D Find the volume of this container.
   E Tell how the volume has changed.

1. A cylindrical container has a diameter of 4 in.
    and a height of 3 in.

   A   B _____

                                          _____

                                          _____

                                          _____

2. Change the diameter of the container to 8 in.

   C   D _____

                                            _____

                                          _____

                                          _____

   E _____

Name _____

Translations and 3-Dimensional Figures

1. Plot the points.
   $A\,(^-2, 2)$; $B\,(3, ^-1)$; $C\,(^-3, ^-1)$.

2. Connect the points in order.

3. Draw the slide image $A'B'C$
   (4 right, 3 up).

4. Draw a line from A to A', B to B' and
   C to C'.

5. What type of figure have you made?

   _____

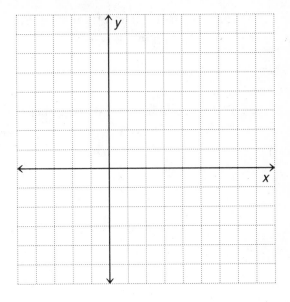

6. Plot the points.
   $A\,(^-2, ^-2)$; $B\,(^-2, 1)$; $C\,(1, 1)$; $D\,(1, 2)$.

7. Connect the points in order.

8. Draw the slide image $A'B'C'D'$
   (2 right, 1 up).

9. Draw segments AA', BB', CC', DD'.

10. What type of figure have you made?

    _____

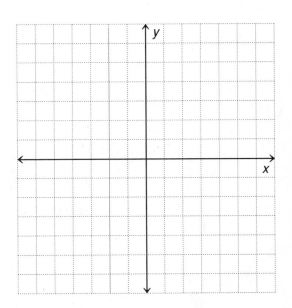

Designs

Use the figures at the right and figures congruent to them to create a design in the box below.

When you have finished your design, compare your method for building the design to other students' methods. Did you add one shape to another or did you proceed differently? Explain.

_____

_____

Assuming Correctly

Describe the cuts that support each assumption.

1.

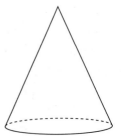

There is 1 way to divide this figure into 2

equal parts. _____

_____

_____

_____

_____

_____

2.

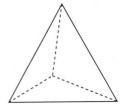

This figure can be divided into 2 equal parts 6

ways. _____

_____

_____

_____

3.

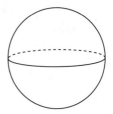

There are an unlimited number of ways to
divide this figure into 4 equal parts.

_____

_____

_____

_____

_____

_____

_____

_____

More or Less

Estimate the answer to each problem. Before finding the actual answer, decide if your estimate is more or less than the actual answer. Ring **more** or **less**. Then find the answer and check if you are right.

1. At the town sports store a basketball costs $22.45 and a volleyball costs $18.79. The coach bought 7 basketballs and 10 volleyballs. How much did he spend?

Estimate: _____   more   less

Answer: _____

2. Last year Kirby had 176 mm of rain in July, 136 mm in August, and 184 mm in September. What was the total rainfall for the 3 months?

Estimate: _____   more   less

Answer: _____

3. Marcella went shopping with $300. She bought a coat for $187.27 and a dress for $48.72. How much money does Marcella have left?

Estimate: _____   more   less

Answer: _____

4. In the school elections Jackie got 379 votes, Elvin got 186 votes and Rafael got 227 votes. How many students voted ?

Estimate: _____   more   less

Answer: _____

5. Judy's checking account had a balance of $247.58. She deposited a check for $36.50. She then withdrew $72.14. How much money is now in her account?

Estimate: _____   more   less

Answer: _____

6. The San Jose camera club had 125 new members in 1988, 135 new members in 1989, and 123 new members in 1990. What was the total number of new members over the 3 years?

Estimate: _____   more   less

Answer: _____

7. Choose one of the problems above and describe how you decided whether the actual answer was more or less than your estimate.

_____

_____

_____

Name _____

Puzzling Expressions

Arrange the numbers from each cloud to give the answer shown.

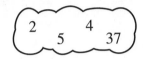

1. _____ + _____ × _____ − _____ = 43

2. _____^{2} + _____ • _____ = 54

3. (_____ + _____) • (_____ − _____) = 32

4. (_____ − _____)^3 + _____ • _____ = 37

5. (_____ • _____) − _____^{3} + _____ = 105

6. (_____ • _____)^2 − (_____ • _____)^3 = 136

Rewrite each expression. Use parentheses to give the answer shown.

7. $4^2 \cdot 2 + 3 - 1$

_____ = 79

8. $16 \cdot 12 - 3^4 + 12$

_____ = 99

9. $5^2 - 5 + 2$

_____ = 18

10. $8 \cdot 9 + 3 - 5^2$

_____ = 71

11. $19 - 3 \cdot 5 + 7$

_____ = 192

12. $7 - 2 \cdot 3 + 5^2$

_____ = 26

13. $2 \cdot 4 - 9 \div 3 + 2$

_____ = 7

14. $6^2 + 2^3 - 3^2 \cdot 4$

_____ = 32

15. $12 \cdot 9 - 3 + 7^2$

_____ = 56

16. $34 - 5^2 + 2 - 3$

_____ = 4

17. $5 - 7 \cdot 1 + 4^2 - 13$

_____ = 1

18. $3^3 - 24 \div 3 \cdot 2$

_____ = 11

Baseball Fever

Janice is writing an article for the school newspaper about this year's baseball team. Janice has made the article a guessing game. Read the article and write an equation. Use Guess and Check to solve.

1. Eight members of this year's baseball team are seventh graders. This is 4 more than twice the number of members that are eighth graders. How many eighth graders are on the baseball team?

_____

2. The baseball team will play 12 home games this season. This is 28 less than 5 times the number of away games. How many away games does the team play this season?

_____

3. The student government runs a concession stand during each home game. The total amount taken in was $360. It made $140 selling drinks. The other item sold was pizza at $1.25 a slice. How many slices did the stand sell?

_____

4. At today's home game, the concession stand took in $162 less than 3 times the amount it took in last year at this time. It made $240 today. How much money did the concession stand make at last year's game?

_____

5. The baseball team needs to raise $780 for new uniforms and equipment. The cost of the new equipment is $360. There are 14 members on the team. How much does each new uniform cost?

_____

6. The baseball team washed cars to raise money. Billy washed 16 cars. This was 12 less than 4 times as many cars as Tony washed. How many cars did Tony wash?

_____

Name _____

Flowing Expressions

A computer flowchart can be used to build and undo expressions.

Look at the expression $7x - 2 = 19$. The flowcharts below show how to undo (solve) and build (check) this expression.

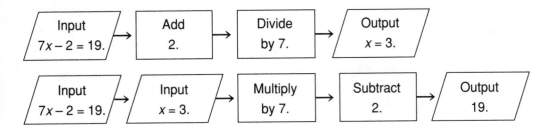

Use flowcharts to build and undo each expression.

1. $3n - 3 = 15$

2. $\dfrac{m}{9} - 2 = 3$

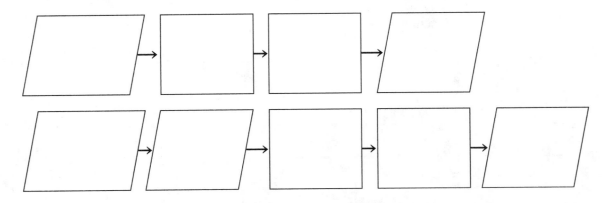

Name _____

Write About It

Write an equation for each sentence. Solve and check
the equation.

1. Five more than 10 times a number is 15.
What is the number?

_____

2. Four less than 2 times a number is ⁻10.
What is the number?

_____

3. The product of ⁻8 and a number is added
to 5 to get ⁻35. What is the number?

_____

4. Subtract 4 from the product of 5 and a
number to get ⁻24. What is the number?

_____

5. Add 12 to ⁻4 times a number.
You get ⁻8. What is the number?

_____

6. Subtract 1 from 15 times a number.
You get 5. What is the number?

_____

7. Add 10 to a number divided by ⁻2.
You get 8. What is the number?

_____

8. Subtract 11 from a number divided by 6.
You get ⁻10. What is the number?

_____

9. If you add 1 to the quotient of a number
divided by 8, you get 10. What is the
number?

_____

10. If you subtract 1 from $\frac{1}{8}$ of an integer,
you get 1. What is the number?

_____

11. Write you own math sentence. Ask a classmate to write the appropriate equation.

_____

_____

_____

_____

Equation: _____

Name _____

The Function Machine

Fill in the missing parts of each function machine.

1.

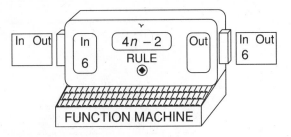

In Out

In 6 | 4n − 2 RULE | Out | In Out 6

2.

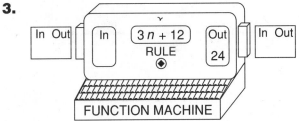

In Out

In | n ÷ 9 RULE | Out 3 | In Out 3

3.

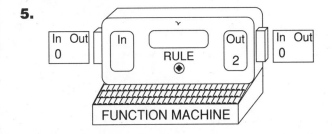

In Out

In | 3n + 12 RULE | Out 24 | In Out

4.

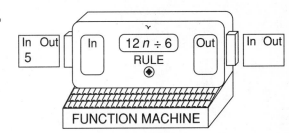

In Out 5

In | 12n ÷ 6 RULE | Out | In Out

5.

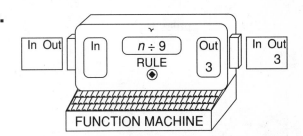

In Out 0

In | RULE | Out 2 | In Out 0

6.

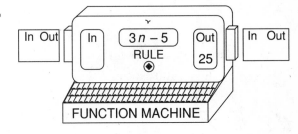

In Out

In | 3n − 5 RULE | Out 25 | In Out

7.

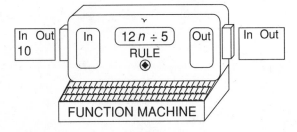

In Out 10

In | 12n ÷ 5 RULE | Out | In Out

8.

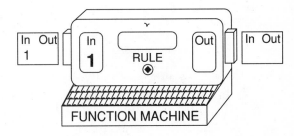

In Out 1

In 1 | RULE | Out | In Out

Apple Math

Write the inequality or equation. Make its graph.
Use the letter after each sentence as the variable.

1. We sell apples for as little as $0.49 per pound and for as much as $0.89 per pound. *s*

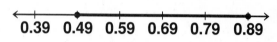

_____

2. We have an agreement to buy apples for $0.40 per pound year-round. *a*

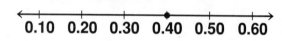

_____

3. The least profit per pound that we make on apples is $0.09. *p*

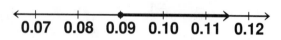

_____

4. Apples are delivered to our store no less than once a week. *d*

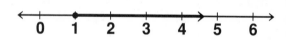

_____

5. No more than 2 apples in each basket of 24 apples may have bruises. *b*

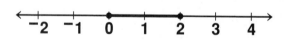

_____

6. We refill our display cases more than twice a day. *r*

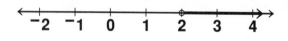

_____

7. Because business is so good, we have less than 1 hour free for lunch. *l*

_____

Name _____

Inequalities and Absolute Value

Recall the following rules for absolute value ($|\ |$), the magnitude of a number without its sign.

If $a > 0$, then $|a| = a$.
If $a < 0$, then $|a| = {}^{-}a$.

Tell whether each statement is always true. Write at least 1 example to support your answer.

1. If $a < 0$ and $b < 0$, then $|a| < |b|$.

_____

2. If $a > 0$ and $b > 0$, then $|a| > |b|$.

_____

3. If $a < 0$ and $b > 0$, then $|a| \geq |b|$.

_____

4. If $a > 0$ and $b > 0$, then $|a| + |b| > 0$.

_____

5. If $a > 0$ and $b < 0$, then $|a| + |b| > 0$.

_____

6. If $a > 0$ and $b > 0$, then $|a + b| > 0$.

_____

7. If $a > 0$ and $b < 0$, then $|a + b| < 0$.

_____

Name _____

Finding Equivalent Expressions

For two expressions to be equivalent, they must have the same answer for any value given of x. In each chart, only two of the expressions are equivalent. Complete each chart and circle the equivalent expressions.

1.

x	$2 + 2x + 4 + 3x$	$x + 3 + 3x + 2$	$5(x + 1) + 1$
1	**11**	**9**	**11**
4	**26**	**21**	**26**
$^-2$	**$^-4$**	**$^-3$**	**$^-4$**

2.

x	$2(x + 1) + 3(2x + 2)$	$8(x + 1)$	$3x + 4 + 5x + 2$
3	**32**	**32**	**30**
8	**72**	**72**	**70**
$^-6$	**$^-40$**	**$^-40$**	**$^-42$**

3.

x	$2(4x + 9)$	$2(4x + 5) + 7$	$x + 14 + 3x + 4x + 3$
10	**98**	**97**	**97**
$^-6$	**$^-30$**	**$^-31$**	**$^-31$**
3	**42**	**41**	**41**

4.

x	$(6x + 2) + (3x + 5)$	$2(x + 3) + 7x + 1$	$4(x + 1) + 5(x + 2)$
0	**7**	**7**	**14**
10	**97**	**97**	**104**
$^-5$	**$^-38$**	**$^-38$**	**$^-31$**

Who Needs a Calculator?

Find the decimal equivalents for the fractions below.
Use a calculator until you recognize a pattern. How
many of these decimal equivalents were you able to
give without using the calculator?

1. $\frac{1}{11}$ = _____

2. $\frac{2}{11}$ = _____

3. $\frac{3}{11}$ = _____

4. $\frac{4}{11}$ = _____

5. $\frac{5}{11}$ = _____

6. $\frac{6}{11}$ = _____

7. $\frac{7}{11}$ = _____

8. $\frac{8}{11}$ = _____

9. $\frac{9}{11}$ = _____

10. $\frac{10}{11}$ = _____

11. $\frac{11}{11}$ = _____

12. $\frac{12}{11}$ = _____

13. $\frac{13}{11}$ = _____

14. $\frac{14}{11}$ = _____

15. $\frac{15}{11}$ = _____

16. $\frac{16}{11}$ = _____

17. $\frac{17}{11}$ = _____

18. $\frac{18}{11}$ = _____

19. $\frac{19}{11}$ = _____

20. $\frac{20}{11}$ = _____

21. $\frac{21}{11}$ = _____

22. $\frac{22}{11}$ = _____

Chord Count

A chord is a line segment that joins 2 points on a circle. In the examples below, n equals the number of chords. Tell what n equals in each example.

1.

$n =$ _____

2.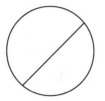

$n =$ _____

3.

$n =$ _____

4.

$n =$ _____

5.

$n =$ _____

6.

$n =$ _____

The chords in Examples 1 through 6 are drawn to form the most regions possible in each circle. In the table below, R equals the number of regions formed by the chords. Complete the table. Use inductive reasoning from number patterns to find R when it becomes too difficult to draw the chords.

7.

n	0	1	2	3	4	5	6	7	8
R									

Use with text pages 458–459.

Locker Madness!

When the new Stompers Middle School opened, the principal, Mr. Parley, challenged the students with a problem at the first assembly. He said, "This year at Stompers we have 1,000 new lockers and 1,000 students. As you know, each student is assigned a locker, and the lockers are numbered 1 to 1,000. Tomorrow morning at 8 a.m. I would like the first student here to open every locker. The second will follow and close every even numbered locker. Next, the third student will open every third locker that is closed and close every third locker that is open. The fourth student will then close every fourth locker that is open and open every fourth locker that is closed.

We will continue in this manner until either every student has had a turn or until someone can predict correctly which lockers would be open if every student did take a turn."

As a loud groan filled the gymnasium, Patti Presto raised her hand and said, "That will be unnecessary, Mr. Parley. I can give you your answer right now." And she did. Patti solved the problem by thinking about only 16 students and 16 lockers.

Use the group of numbers below to help you think about the first 16 lockers that are opened and closed by the first 16 students. Then use what you discover to predict which of the 1,000 lockers will remain open

$$\begin{array}{cccc} 1 & 2 & 3 & 4 \\ 5 & 6 & 7 & 8 \\ 9 & 10 & 11 & 12 \\ 13 & 14 & 15 & 16 \end{array}$$

_____

_____

_____

_____

_____

_____

_____

_____

_____

_____

_____

Dazzling Digits

Try each number trick or puzzle below. Then write the
steps that show why each trick works or how you
solved the puzzle.

1. Choose any number and multiply it by 4. Add half
of the product. Add half of this sum. Divide by 9.
Do you have the number you began with?

_____

2. Pick any number. Add 6 and multiply the result by 3.
Subtract 18. Multiply by 2. Divide by 6. Do you have
the number you chose at the beginning?

_____

3. Think of a number and double it. Add 5. Multiply the
sum by 10. Subtract 50 and divide by 10. Take half of
that. Do you end where you started?

_____

4. The sum of a number and the number doubled is 30.
What is the number?

_____

5. The sum of 2 numbers is 5. One number is 4 times the
other. What are the two numbers?

_____

6. One number is 6 more than the other. The sum of the
two numbers is 12. What are the two numbers?

_____

Prove It

Use math reasoning to prove formulas you have
learned about the figures below.

1. The diagram of the triangle shows that the
sum of the angles of a triangle is 180°. Show how to use
the diagram of the quadrilateral in a similar way to
show that the sum of its angles is 360°.

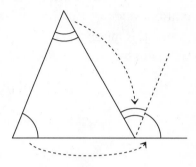

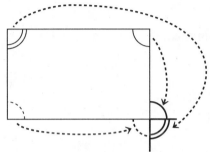

2. Add one line to the diagram at the right to show
another way to prove that the sum of the angles of
a quadrilateral is 360° .

Explain: _____

_____

_____

_____

_____

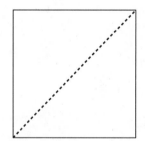

3. Use a similar method to show why the formula for
the area of a parallelogram, $A = b \times h$, is the same as
the formula for the area of a rectangle.

Explain: _____

_____

_____

_____

_____

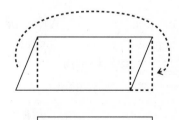

Logically Speaking

1. Read the statement. Then put a check by each of the
conditions under which Randolph could go to the movies.
<u>Statement</u>: Randolph can go to the movies only if it is
raining and he has enough money.

Conditions: _____ It is raining. He has enough money.

_____ It is raining. He does not have enough money.

_____ It is not raining. He has enough money.

_____ It is not raining. He does not have enough money.

2. Read the statement. Then put a check by the conditions
under which Julie would not go to school.
<u>Statement</u>: Julie never goes to school if she has a fever
or it is a holiday.

Conditions: _____ She has a fever. It is a holiday.

_____ She has a fever. It is not a holiday.

_____ She has no fever. It is a holiday.

_____ She has no fever. It is not a holiday.

3. Read the statement. Write the 4 possible combinations of conditions.
Then put a check by the ones under which Erin will score 100%.
<u>Statement</u>: Erin will score 100% on the test if she spells all
the words correctly and writes an appropriate definition for each.

_____ _____

_____ _____

_____ _____

_____ _____

Logic Chains

If . . . then statements can be chained together to make
new logical inferences. Write the conclusion by
chaining the statements.

1. If Mr. Smitz sells his house, he will buy Mrs. Godel's. If Mr. Smitz
buys Mrs. Godel's house, Mrs. Godel will move to Mexico.

_____

_____

2. If John loads the dishwasher, the dirty dishes will get clean.
If John runs the dishwasher, Megan will put away the clean dishes.

_____

_____

3. If Fred lets his dog Fifi off the leash, she runs away. If Fifi
runs away, Fred's mother phones all the neighbors.

_____

_____

4. If Suzi gets the baby-sitting job, she will stop at the car wash.
If Suzi goes to the car wash, her car will be clean.

_____

_____

5. If the dentist finds that Justin has no cavities, his mother will treat
him to a movie. If Justin's mother treats Justin to a movie, his dad
will work late.

_____

_____

6. If there is rain for 5 days in a row, the river will rise. If the river
rises, Shirley will go rafting next Saturday.

_____

_____

Story Line

Graph the following story. Label the events on the graph.

A Jan quickly pedaled his bike to reach top speed on the straightaway.

B Even at the bottom of steep Hillcrest Road, he maintained his speed for a little while.

C Then his speed dropped as quickly as he had built it up originally.

D By the time he reached the top of the hill, he was pedaling at only 10% of his top speed.

E Exhausted, he stopped to rest for a few minutes.

F He gradually started off again.

G He pedaled home at half his top speed.

Create your own story. Ask a classmate to make the graph.

_____

_____

_____

_____

_____

_____

_____

_____

_____

Puzzle Pairs

Find the pairs of puzzles. Remember to use similar strategies for related problems.

1. Place the numbers 1 to 11 in the circles so that the 3 numbers in each line add to 18.

Problems 1 and _____ are related.

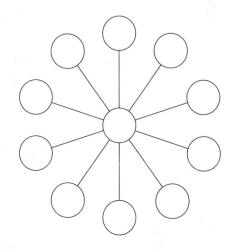

3. I am a prime 2-digit number. The sum of my digits is divisible by 4. The product of my digits is less than 5. Who am I?

Problems 4 and _____ are related.

Answer: _____

5. Five girls swam a 200-meter race. Tina came in first. Joy came in last. If Amber was ahead of Misty, and Grace was behind her, who came in second?

Problems 5 and _____ are related.

Answer: _____

2. I am divisible by 5 and less than 4 digits. I am odd, and the sum of my digits is a square number. I am greater than 12 x 12. The product of my digits is 15. Who am I?

Problems 2 and _____ are related.

Answer: _____

4. Five people were standing in a row. My only sister was standing between her brother-in-law and his brother-in-law. My sister's husband, who is an only child, was standing next to his sister-in-law. She was standing 2 places away from my brother. Who am I, and where was I standing?

Problems 4 and _____ are related.

Answer: _____

_____

_____

_____

6. Arrange the numbers 1 to 9 in the grid so that the sum is 15 when the digits are added horizontally, vertically, and diagonally.

Problems 6 and _____ are related.

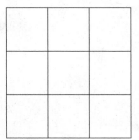